ALL IS GRACE

ALL IS GRACE

The Spirituality of
Dorothy Day

William D. Miller

DOUBLEDAY & COMPANY, INC.
GARDEN CITY, NEW YORK
1987

BX
4705
.D283
M53
1987

Library of Congress Cataloging-in-Publication Data
Miller, William D., 1916–
    All is grace.
    Includes index.
    1. Day, Dorothy, 1897– —Diaries. 2. Day,
Dorothy, 1897– —Correspondence. 3. Catholics—
United States—Biography. 4. Spirituality—Catholic
Church—History—20th century. 5. Catholic Church—
Doctrines—History—20th century. I. Title.
BX4705.D283M53   1987   267'.182'0924 [B]   86–16628
ISBN 0-385-23429-5

Dedicated to Sister Leo Marie Preher, O.P.

Contents

Introduction

It was in April, 1975, that I got a letter from Dorothy Day, dated April 10. "Dear Bill," she began. "Here I am sorting out more note-books to be ready for your visit." After mentioning her ailments, she went on to speak of a book she was reading and of the author's writing style. As for her own writing, she was doing little. "I feel I have written plenty," she said. Then she added what to me was a rather enigmatic statement: "With your help," she wrote, "I could have another book with little effort." She never said what she meant by "another book," and I never asked. With Dorothy it was better to let whatever was in her mind live or die in due course.

She was clear on one point. She wanted me to visit her as soon as I could while she was out at her little beach cottage on Staten Island. As I recall, I got there about two weeks later. During my first day there we toured the area, visiting here and there the places that had been a part of her life when, as a young woman, she had first come to the Island. At each one we lingered briefly, long enough for her to indulge her memories.

Rather formally, she assigned the next afternoon at two o'clock for our work meeting. Though it struck me as curious that she would "set up" a meeting for her business, it was right at the minute when I took the backyard path to her place from the nearby cottage where I had spent the night and where her friend, Marge Hughes, and Marge's son, Johnny, were staying. Without preliminary pleasantries —she was grim, in fact—she addressed the matter at hand. I was to be seated. She would stand. For at least an hour she talked about events in her past life that she had tried to suppress because, as she said, she detested the element of sensationalism that would be at-tached to them were they to be made public. Besides, she was afraid that some might say, Well, Dorothy Day was a real cut-up—she had had her fun, why not they? She talked of people she had hurt and of others who had hurt her by accusing her of unspeakable things. She did not name her detractors, saying only that she probably deserved the pain they had caused her because she had been arrogant and overbearing toward them.

As she talked, I, ill at ease, kept hoping that some all-sufficient and even healing remark would moderate the tension and put her more at ease. As it was, she seemed almost to be suffering. Her face was white and drawn, and most of the time her gaze was directed at something far away. My appropriate comments never came. I was mute. Finally, she finished and walked into an adjacent room and brought out three books, which she gave to me. One was her autobiographical *The Eleventh Virgin*, published by Liveright in 1924, and the other two were books in which she figured: Agnes Boulton's *Part of a Long Story* and Caroline Gordon's *The Malefactors*. She commented only on *The Eleventh Virgin*. The principal events in the book, including the abortion episode, were true, she said. How did she feel about that? she asked herself. She said she could not say. Her face was hard-set and she stared out of the back window for a moment. Then she directed my attention to some boxes on the floor. She said that she had had an impulse many times to burn all of the papers in the boxes. But she had not—she could not burn anything—and I was to take them and do with them whatever I chose: burn them, if I thought they ought to be burned. I would burn nothing, I said. I would go through all the material, piece by piece, and then put it in the Catholic Worker archives at Marquette University. And that is what happened, down to the last scrap of paper. Before this was done, however, Dorothy had asked that my daughter, Carol Miller, transcribe all of her handwritten journals into typescript so that she might have a typewritten copy. Carol did this, and from Carol's copy I made one for myself.

As I went through her papers over the year—1975—I found two book-length manuscripts: one on Peter Maurin and the other, a collection of retreat notes and spiritual reflections which she had entitled "All Is Grace." Both manuscripts were so roughly put together that they were, as manuscripts, beyond reconstruction. At first I was concerned with the Maurin manuscript, in part because Dorothy had from the first urged me to write about Maurin. Maybe she emphasized him to de-emphasize herself; I had already told her that I wanted to do her biography, a proposition which she staunchly resisted. On the other hand, I could not but agree with her that Maurin was, as she said many times, a transcending figure, spiritually and intellectually. But Maurin had had his biographer in Arthur Sheehan, and, insofar as the facts of Maurin's life were concerned, little more of significance could be added.

Of much more personal concern to her was the "All Is Grace" manuscript. This came from her wanting to tell of her religious retreat experiences over the years of World War II, because in the course of her life of reaching for God this period had seemed to her to be the most luminous. As she thought of the retreats, she realized that they had afforded her a vision of the transcendent destiny of all life and had given her the strength to pursue this vision. She fretted about this intended book for nearly forty years. Sometime during World War II she noted: "Help me O my God to write about these joys of the spiritual life." In her journal entry of June 27, 1967, she told of "trying to write. 2 pages, no more and I awake wondering how I can possibly get that book done. Then I . . . remember my promise . . . to write about the retreat, and must toil on." Father John Hugo, about whom more will be said later, recalled that Dorothy had "many times" stated her intention of writing a book about the spiritual awakening that she had known during the war years, but never had because, as she said, she "did not feel equipped to write on theology."

Perhaps. Still, among her papers was the three-hundred-page manuscript telling of the ideas and insights that were at the heart of her spiritual formation during this wartime period. Was this what she wanted me to help her with? The only corroborating reason that I can think of is her desperate need to tell about this part of her life. In her view, it was the climax of a glory that had, through the grace of God, lifted her out of the bottomless pit of despair into which her life had once fallen, and had then opened for her "an instruction and way of life," in the Church. Then she had been given a "work," for as her teacher, Peter Maurin, had made her see, it was in the light of this glory that all of creation should lie; for creation had fallen into darkness.

Still, there was one thing more that she wanted. As World War II began, she, herself, sought to be girded with an inner strength and final assurance that she might remain steadfast and give a good account of herself in her own war, as it were. She found that strength and assurance in the spiritual retreats that she began just as World War II broke out. Almost immediately, she found in the retreats a source of the strength she sought. In notes that she kept at this time she wrote: "I have always been so sure I was right, that I was being led by God—that is in the main outlines of my life, that I confidently expected Him to show His will by external events. And I looked for some big happening, some unmistakable sign. I disregarded all the little signs. I begin now to see them and with such clearness that I have to beg not to be shown too much, for fear I cannot bear it. I need strength to do what I have to do—strength and joy and peace and vision. Lord, that I may see! That prayer is certainly most overwhelmingly answered on this retreat."

For the remainder of her life the "vision" was all that mattered to her. She wrote of it in the *Catholic Worker* for almost half a century and she told of it in the thousands of talks she gave over the years. But somehow the story was never given the focus that would let others see the real source of her passion. She was written about, exclaimed over, and applauded for her uncompromising stands on social issues, especially when they seemed to confound princes and prelates. This emphasis on herself truly dismayed her. Her person was not the light. It was grace that had brought her into the light, and it was of this that she wanted to write. Her fundamental conviction, on which all her ideas of a new earth were based, was that to love was to bring the reality of God into life. If she was simpleminded in believing that it was an abortion of love to think that a little preemptive violence here and there could preserve and magnify love, then simplicity, some might say, is the prescription that is now needed.

I do not know why she never finished her book, and she may not have been thinking of it when she wrote me in April 1975. All I know is that in May of that year, she gave me the manuscript that she had never finished.

I do not in my work here presume to finish hers. If Dorothy suffered from an inadequacy in her knowledge of theology, then I certainly have no business trying to give proportion and refinement to her manuscript. I am convinced, however, that the sifting and sorting that may be a part of theological professionalism has little to add to her three hundred pages. Aside from the interior truth of her reflections, their significance comes from the perspective of history. As statements of what she regarded as truths in the life of the spirit, they represent a radical confrontation with the character of contemporary life. It is in these reflections that the radicalism of Dorothy Day is found—not in demonstrating on the picket line, not in standing before a judge, not in languishing behind the bars of a cell.

In "All Is Grace" Dorothy stated that her objective was to convey a "taste" of what she had found to be the transforming truths of the life of the spirit. In an attempt to achieve this end, my own approach has been to extract, in her own words, segments of her reflections and to reorganize them under appropriate thematic headings. The collection that has resulted will, I hope, be interesting and edifying because of the informed character of her spirituality and the impact of truth which it registers.

Beyond their intrinsic interest, these spiritual reflections rise to a new plane of meaning when placed in the context of history. When seen against this background they constitute the basis of Dorothy's radicalism, becoming, in fact, a revolutionary document in that they proclaim a level of existence infinitely above today's flat and fearfully autocratic patterns.

In my Introduction to these expressions of Dorothy's spirituality I have tried to give, in terms of the sources of her own intellectual formation, a character to what can be termed her confrontation of history. It is in this position that she is unique to our time. I have also included a biographical segment, providing such substance as may help one understand why she called her manuscript "All Is Grace."

Through the goodwill and generosity of three of Dorothy's closest friends, Sister Peter Claver Fahy, Father Leo Neudecker, and Nina Polcyn Moore, I am able to conclude this book with a third section, a selection of letters that Dorothy wrote to them over the last fifteen years of her life. Dorothy was heavy-burdened during this period with physical infirmities and woes of the world that seemed to fall upon her with a selective vehemence. But, as these letters show, she was still filled with faith, hope, charity, and the joy of living.

Part One

DOROTHY DAY AND THE WEAPONS OF THE SPIRIT

1

Dorothy Day

She was born on November 8, 1897, at Bath Beach, Brooklyn. Her mother, Grace Satterlee, from a Marlboro, New York, family of merchants and seamen, was the daughter of a Civil War veteran who had been wounded and then, while still in the service, had contracted tuberculosis. He was a semi-invalid for the rest of his short life. Dorothy's father, John I. Day, was a Southerner, from Cleveland, Tennessee. His family background was Scotch-Irish and, of course, Presbyterian, although some of the family had become Campbellites. This defection caused some consternation within the Presbyterian branch and, in the case of John Day, much bitterness. The defectors, conspicuously "religious," were also the well-to-do but tight-fisted, and when it came to a distribution of their endowments, all went to the church with nothing for the upkeep and betterment of the ambitious and deserving old-line family members—like young, bound-to-succeed John Day.

Any wound to him seemed never to heal and it is likely he declared himself an atheist, and stuck by this declaration for most of his life, as a response to what he regarded as the smug religiosity of his comfortable family members. This aura of the hurt and embittered man, which he seemed to have perpetually worn, made some people think of him as gruff and surly. Two constants in his life testified to beauty and goodness. One was his fascination for the sight of a moving horse, so he chose the racetracks when he decided to become a newspaper reporter. So incisive was his discernment in predicting which steed would perform best on a given day that he was known, among those who lived within the special comradeship of horse fanciers, as "Judge" Day. The other constant and cohering element in his life was his wife, Grace. An immensely attractive woman, according to a picture of her taken after her marriage, she was John Day's Eros. Her character was marked by strength and stability, and all of its elements were used to uphold her husband and her family.

Dorothy's more obvious traits came from her father. She looked like him, fair and large-boned. She had his quick intelligence and his appreciation of good literature. Once her mind was set she could be as hard and unyielding as he. But there was one difference. If John Day appeared palsied by the question of existence, his daughter was driven by an almost ruthless passion to find an answer. Whatever element of temperament or circumstance stood at this point of separation between the two, it kept them apart and at odds with one another for the rest of John Day's life. He was rooted in the traditions and even the prejudices of the area in which he had been reared, and, except for his attitude toward religion, he seemed to have moved not one whit away from them. Dorothy rebelled against them and searched, with what to him seemed a reckless abandon, for a new meaning on which to base her life.

John Day had met Grace Satterlee in New York, where she, like John, was attending business school. Each found in the other compelling reasons to enter into a marriage contract. Two children, Sam and Donald, came before Dorothy, and two more, Della and John, after.

When Dorothy was six, the family moved to Oakland, California, where Day wrote of horses and horse racing for a local newspaper. When the great earthquake of 1906 destroyed the plant that produced the newspaper, Day immediately moved his family to Chicago. For about a year, living in a row tenement, the family struggled to survive. Day, unemployed and convinced that he could put his track lore into a book that would make the family prosperous, put all his energy into writing. But nothing came of it, and, finally, he got a job reporting track news for the Chicago *Inter-Ocean*. After this the family moved to a better location.

In her two autobiographical books—*From Union Square to Rome,* published in 1939, and *The Long Loneliness,* brought out some fifteen years later—Dorothy writes of the years of her girlhood in Chicago with a warmth and openness that do not mark her writings about other parts of her life. Her teenage years were given over to taking care of her baby brother, John, on whom she doted, and doing housework. Her closest companion was her sister, Della, and it was a tie that lasted throughout their lives.

Aside from her family, her other love was reading. In enjoining this old-fashioned custom upon his daughter, John Day could not have served her better—or to her greater satisfaction. As he supervised and encouraged her in this habit, she fulfilled all of his hopes for her and better. On winter nights, long after the others had gone to bed, she would sit by the coal fire, studying her Latin and Greek, and then, when her homework was done, she would luxuriate for several hours more with a book.

When she was fifteen, she won a Hearst newspaper scholarship competition enabling her to go to the University of Illinois. Her first year was an unhappy one. She was desperately homesick and hardpressed financially. Her first job was setting tables in the dining hall of the Young Women's Christian Association. In things like dances, football games, and sororities, she had no part at all. And however she might rationalize their absence, she was still a fifteen-year-old girl and she missed them. Her defense against the hurt of social exclusion was to take on manners that would flaunt her imperviousness to what others thought. She began to smoke, she affected crude speech, and she spoke critically of campus religious organizations. She joined the Socialist Club, and, with all of it, lost her table-setting job.

In 1916 the Day family moved to New York, where Day had been offered a job as a sports editor on the New York *Morning Telegraph.* Dorothy went with the family, but not just to remain with it. She had had enough of college and she saw New York as the place to begin her big adventure—whatever it was. She had long since decided that her work was to be in journalism, like her father's. John Day was adamantly opposed to the idea, convinced that a woman journalist could be only one step away from harlotry. If Dorothy persisted in this madness, he decreed, she should have no bed in his house.

She left almost blithely. Thinking, perhaps, to pressure Dorothy back into the household, Day asked his friends in journalism not to hire her and to urge her to forego her ambition. But Dorothy executed what might be termed an "end run." After a number of fruitless applications with the established newspapers, she went to the office of the Socialist *Call,* on the Lower East Side, and wheedled a job from Chester Wright, the reluctant editor.

She worked there for about eight months, making five dollars a week. Her work brought her into the predominantly Jewish Lower East Side, a place to which she would refer ever after as her true home. Her writing for the *Call* was not noteworthy, but she savored the bohemian-like existence that went with her work. Usually she stayed at the *Call* office until the early morning hours, putting together the paper, and then sat out the night in some all-night eatery, chain-smoking, drinking coffee, and discussing the latest books and those revolutionary changes in thought and society that were beginning to flare the world over. Her companions were normally Mike Gold, the assistant editor, and whoever else might drop in from the ragtag bohemia of the Village. They talked until the sun, having some five hours earlier passed over the battlefields of Europe, lowered its first light on the East River. Then, when the morning mists could first be seen passing along the street, she would go to whatever out-of-the-way backstreet room she happened to have for the moment and sleep through the morning.

She left the *Call* in the early months of 1917. She left, apparently, because of a falling-out she had had with Gold. They had been "going together," as it was called then. But Mike, who in the thirties would edit the Communist *Daily Worker,* came to find that Dorothy was headstrong and bent on a course of her own, wherever it lay.

For the moment her course lay in the organization of some Columbia University students who wanted to oppose America's entry into World War I. In late March a protest caravan left New York for Washington, accompanied by Dorothy as a "news correspondent." There were rallies and confrontations with the police, and sometimes these confrontations were violent. She found the violence abhorrent and she recognized that, at least in one instance, a kind of mob self-righteousness on the part of the students invited police intervention. The group arrived in Washington just as President Wilson was declaring war on Germany.

Back in New York, Dorothy became the editor of *The Masses,* a kind of upstart journal dedicated to lampooning capitalist bourgeois morality and affirming the vision of revolutionary causes a-borning in the world. Max Eastman had been the editor, and Floyd Dell his assistant. Both were "on leave" during the summer of 1917, mainly because the journal's days were numbered. The government's legal machinery was already working to suppress it, and Dell chose Dorothy to attend its dying moments and arrange the obsequies.

In November, out of work, Dorothy was persuaded by her friend Peggy Baird to go to Washington to join a group of suffragettes who planned to picket the White House. She went more for the promised excitement than for the cause, since she doubted that the enfranchisement of women would do much for changing the world for the better. Excitement there was. The women were arrested and imprisoned, and when the warden laid hands on Dorothy to take her to a cell she retaliated in a passion of biting and kicking. For this she was placed in solitary confinement. It was not a condition that she bore well. A sense of the utter helplessness of her situation came upon her with crushing force. What was she doing there? What had her life amounted to? And, more than ever, she felt the conviction that there was something for her to do. But what?

The solitary confinement was only for a few days. President Wilson pardoned the women so that they could be home for their Thanksgiving dinners. For Dorothy, there was no family dinner. She and Peggy ate at a Washington restaurant, and then they took the train back to New York and the Village.

She found some part-time work with Max Eastman, but it was of small importance, and even in the last years of her life she recalled with distaste how she would take his office mail to his house on Washington Square. She lived precariously, staying with whoever of her friends might have a place for her to sleep.

But her nights made up for the dreariness of the days. One evening she went with Mike Gold to the Provincetown Playhouse on MacDougal Street, and there Gold introduced her to Eugene O'Neill. She may have fancied his glowing eyes and sunken cheeks, and perhaps thought she might replace the gall in his soul with honey. But in those night-long sessions, as she sat with him in the back room of Jimmy Wallace's "Golden Swan," he gave her something of greater substance than a trembling hand to hold or a recitation of his misspent youth. When O'Neill heard Dorothy's own story of her restlessness and of the call she sometimes felt she heard from God, he urged her to read St. Augustine's *Confessions*. It was here, said Father John Hugo at the Dorothy Day Memorial Mass at Marquette University on November 5, 1981, that "she heard the unforgettable words which summarize the whole burden of the saint's story: 'You have made our hearts for yourself, O God, and they will never rest until they rest in you.' "

Late one night in the "hellhole," as Wallace's back room was called, O'Neill, quite drunk, recited Francis Thompson's poem "The Hound of Heaven." "Gene could recite all of it," said Dorothy, in *From Union Square to Rome*. "He used to sit there, looking dour and black, his head sunk on his chest, sighing, 'And now my heart is as a broken fount wherein tear-drippings stagnate.' " It was, she continued, "one of those poems that awaken the soul, recalls to it the fact that God is its destiny. The idea of this pursuit fascinated me, the inevitableness of it, the recurrence of it, made me feel that inevitably I would have to pause in the mad rush of living to remember my first beginning and last end." When she heard O'Neill's recitation, she said, neither O'Neill nor Mike Gold "knew . . . how profoundly moved I was. I did my best to hide it, but I was again 'tormented by God.' "

In the winter of 1918 she lived around the corner from St. Joseph's Catholic Church on Sixth Avenue. Many times, after sitting throughout the night with O'Neill, she would walk home with him and put him to bed, sodden and shivering. Throwing her coat over him, she would lie next to him to give him her warmth, and after his ague had passed she would walk in the early morning light the eight or so blocks to her own room. "Many a morning," she wrote in *The Long Loneliness*, "I went to an early morning Mass at St. Joseph's . . . and knelt in the back of the church, not knowing what was going on at the altar, but warmed and comforted by the lights and silence, the kneeling people and the atmosphere of worship." Why did she do this? "Because I felt again and again the need . . . to kneel, to bow my head in prayer. . . . It was blind instinct . . . it was an act of the will."

The Hound of Heaven pursued her, but still she "fled Him, down the nights and down the days; . . . fled Him down the arches of the years; . . . fled Him down the labyrinthine ways. . . ." For, as Dorothy says in *The Long Loneliness,* "it was the life of the flesh [that] called to me as a good and wholesome life. . . . What was good and what was evil? . . . The satisfied flesh has its own law."

In May 1918, she left her bohemian life to become a nurse trainee in King's County Hospital, Brooklyn. In the hospital she met a man who had been a patient, an egotistical, heavy-drinking, and brawling adventurer whose normal occupation was that of womanizing and, according to Ernest Hemingway, performing prodigies of journalistic output. This was Lionel Moise, the model for Ben Hecht's central character in *The Front Page.* Writer Malcolm Cowley, who knew Moise, characterized him as a man before whom "women prostrated themselves." And Dorothy, twenty-one years old, virginal, and actually without previous serious romantic adventure in her life, positively disintegrated before Moise. Always one to move impetuously, even recklessly, she flung herself at him and then flung herself into his apartment. Six months later she was pregnant, and then, after four months, she had an abortion. Nonetheless, Moise left her.

For the rest of her days this part of her life was kept a secret, around which she erected an impenetrable silence. Even in the closing years of her life only several people knew of it. One was a young woman, pregnant, who had gone to the Catholic Worker house and was thinking of having an abortion. Dorothy wrote her a letter, telling of her own experience and begging her not to subject herself to the suffering that she, Dorothy, had undergone.

The consequences of the abortion were near catastrophic. Ill, she took a room with a German family which, as she later said, treated her with extraordinary compassion. Yet she lived with such desolation that twice she initiated attempts at suicide.

Gradually she built a fantasy: it was that she would again become pregnant and that the lost child would be reincarnated in a new birth. Underlying this statement are some lines in *The Eleventh Virgin* in which she depicts these fantasies. Moreover, her actions in the three years following the abortion certainly uphold this idea.

She married almost immediately. Her husband was Barkeley Tobey, a publisher's idea man, twice Dorothy's age and, according to Malcolm Cowley, a veteran of a number of previous marriages. Theirs was a caricature of a marriage that began with a trip to England and France. For a brief period, perhaps a month or two, Dorothy played out this caricature by doing the extravagant things that disillusioned young American writers were supposed to do when they were in Europe, and, of course, doing so with a special energy when in Paris. But her marriage and the life that went with it seem to have become unbearable, and Dorothy, presumably with consolatory funds provided by her husband, went to Italy. She saw no more of this man—who lived another forty years and who for a few years, at least, remained Dorothy's legal husband.

She stayed six months in Capri, writing *The Eleventh Virgin*. In 1921, or early 1922, she returned to the United States and went almost directly to Chicago. It seems obvious that she went there because Lionel Moise was there, and to follow a fantasy that had become a delirium. For nearly two years she stayed in Chicago, working in one nondescript job and then another, pursuing Moise into the depths of his own abandonment until she recognized, at last, that her dream, where he was concerned, was, and always would be, a nightmare.

In 1923 she went to New Orleans to work as a reporter. Her principal assignment was to pose as a taxi dancer and write sob stories about the "girls," presumably entrapped in this supposedly sordid kind of life. Fortunately, her job did not last long. She had been in New Orleans only several months when she got word from the Liveright publishing house that her manuscript, "The Eleventh Virgin," had been sold to a movie producer and that she would get $2,500 as her part of the transaction.

She apparently stayed in New Orleans only long enough to buy a ticket to New York, where she rejoined her Village companions. First among these was Peggy, now married to Malcolm Cowley.

Peggy, a dabbler in art, could have been (except for not having tuberculosis) the Mimi of a Village *La Bohème*. Peggy was not an intellectual; she was a party girl, vivacious, willowy, and sexually piquant with a touch of the ribald about her. But she loved all living things, beginning with her flowers and cats, and she had been a good friend to Dorothy, having tried to persuade her not to have the abortion. So it was to Peggy and Malcolm and to their companions and friends that Dorothy went.

It was an interesting group of writers and thinkers, among whom were Cowley, the critic; John Dos Passos; and rhetorician Kenneth Burke. Burke had recently married a girl of the Village, Lily Batterham, and she had brought to the company a pale, sandy-haired, and seemingly undernourished young man, recently discharged from an army hospital. This was Forster Batterham, and of course Dorothy fell for him—for, no doubt, Forster's hand, too, trembled a little.

Forster was an anarchist. There was nothing philosophical about his position; he simply wanted no commitments. He liked solitude, he liked to fish, and he liked the beach, so one day Dorothy and Peggy, carrying a circular of advertisements of beach cottages for sale, took the ferry to Staten Island and then the car line down to the island's western and least populated end. There, on the bay, across from the Jersey shore, Dorothy found a place she could afford, a beach house of some three small rooms and a porch. There was a loft upstairs, big enough for a cot and a few pieces of furniture.

It was not much, but what matter? The day was lovely. It was April 1924. In front of the house was the blue of the bay, and at its door complacent waves washed ashore. Behind it the new green of spring covered the trees. Peggy was delighted; she could already see climbing roses for the porch and a garden in the small space outside the back door. Dorothy could see these attractions too, but she could also see Forster fishing in the bay, getting a tan for his pallid countenance and adding flesh to his spare frame. And while Forster fished and collected specimens of marine life, she would read and write the stories and articles from which she would get enough money to set the table and pay the taxes.

So she took what remained of her money and bought the cottage. Was it, in the unspoken areas of its conception, all contrived, to give substance to the desperate hope that she might get pregnant? Very likely it was, but at the heart of it was a commitment to Forster. "I loved him in every way, as a wife and a mother even," she says in *The Long Loneliness.* This special feeling for him continued into her old age—as shown by the pleasure she took from his telephone calls and gifts, and her delight at his having expressed pride in their grandchildren. One morning—it was July 4, 1975—she sat in the bright sun on a small porch outside her room at the Catholic Worker farm at Tivoli, and, in relation to nothing that was being said, she interposed a reflection on the time she had lived with Forster. Once one had shared so vital a part of one's life with another, she said, there could never be any final separation of those two lives.

In *The Long Loneliness* Dorothy tells of an idyllic day in June 1925 when she was certain that she was pregnant. She and Forster, with Peggy and Malcolm, had gone to a circus in Tottenville. They had a picnic lunch with them: "dandelion wine and pickled eels." One assumes, of course, that it was the eels that brought on the classic symptoms. The churning of her stomach and the heavy taste of eels could only confirm her "blissful joy" as she returned that afternoon to the cottage.

When Tamar was born the following March, Dorothy wrote an account of the delivery that was published in *The New Masses,* a new communist journal edited by Mike Gold. It was a curious article for her old friend to publish, since there was not the slightest outcry against any presumed oppression by either God or man in it. Every sentence was heavy with contentment. Heaven and nature sang for Dorothy that summer; and one day, as she wheeled a gurgling Tamar along Hyland Boulevard, she met a nun. Could Sister Aloysia arrange for the child's baptism? Yes, said Sister, nothing loath. In due course it was done.

This turn to religion brought a separation from Forster. It seems likely that she hoped to bring her life into order, to marry him if that could be made acceptable to him, to the state, and even to the Church, for she was still a woman already married. But none of this was for Forster. He could make no final commitment—to Dorothy, God, or anyone. Where he was concerned, Dorothy's preoccupation with religion was a wall between them. He had not wanted her to have Tamar and then he had not wanted Tamar baptized. He began to spend more time in New York City, and when he did return to the beach the tension between them was unbearable. Inevitably, there was a complete break. Two years later, on December 27, 1927, Dorothy was baptized at the church of Our Lady, Help of Christians, at Tottenville, Staten Island.

Her decision had been made deliberately. She had not experienced, even remotely, the billowing wave of piety which was supposed to make joyful those final steps toward religious commitment. But she knew that the Hound of Heaven still pursued her, and always would, and she could run no more.

The next four years in her life were a time of wandering. She took a job as a movie scriptwriter in Hollywood; then, dismayed with the mind and manners of moviemaking, she took Tamar to Mexico City. She lived there very simply, writing articles about herself, Tamar, and the life around them. These were published in *Commonweal* and *America* and earned her enough money on which to live.

She had gone to Mexico to separate herself from the tempests and temptations of her old life in New York, but with the Great Depression settling down on the world, life even in Mexico was becoming increasingly precarious. In the spring of 1932 she returned to New York, settling finally in a small apartment on Fifteenth Street, chosen because it had a small backyard in which Tamar could play. In December she got an assignment from *America* to report a Communist-organized "hunger march" that was to occur in Washington.

At the time, Dorothy had been a Catholic for five years. In the face of every conceivable argument or reason for practicing her religion on the nominal outer edge of her Catholic registration—or even dropping it—she had worked very hard at understanding the form and spirit of the community she had entered. She had lived close to poverty; she had labored to rear her daughter; alone, she had "gone into Egypt" to remove herself from temptation. The Washington experience brought her to a crisis. She was now an "instructed" Catholic. But where was the burning center of her faith? In Washington she saw the stumbling, tattered horde moving down the streets, but what could she give them? It was not only these men but the world that groaned. A darkness was beginning to settle over life, and she wanted to take a light into it. But where and how?

2

Peter Maurin

When Dorothy Day returned to New York from the Washington hunger marches on December 9, 1932, she was met in her small backroom kitchen by a gray-haired man whose greeting was heavily laden with the accents of southern France. This was Peter Maurin, the itinerant worker, the peasant-intellectual. This was the man, Dorothy later said, "whose spirit and ideas [would] dominate . . . the rest of [her] life," the man whom she called a saint and a genius. From almost every standpoint, Peter stood outside or in opposition to the intellectual and value totems of the twentieth century. Like Jacques Maritain and the French personalists, he believed that history had taken an erratic and dangerous turn. A vision of those exalted heights which, according to Christ, were the true destiny of the person had all but been lost to sight, obscured by the attractions of the senses and of power. Peter wanted a culture whose measure was freedom and not the perfection of systems. He wanted a society whose values would give life to the principle of the common unity of people. He believed that the person was primary to the system and that the system alone could not make people good. It was, as Peter continually said, the person, free, creative, and open to a vision of unity and beauty, that would begin to breathe into life a "climate" in which it would "be easier for the other person to be good." It was, therefore, personalist action and not state action that would create a new society.

In this revolutionary reversal of factors required to redirect history toward a true humanism, the idea of a church was crucially essential.

Peter recognized that, in contemporary mass culture, personhood had been chained to the "necessity" of serving the system. And now, he said, the Church should give to people a fresh vision of freedom and beauty. Since the action of the Church in history was to set a standard of beauty and of freedom, it was the son or daughter of the Church who now should strive to bring that standard into life.

Peter gave Dorothy the insight, or "the clarification," as he called it, as to how her religious quest actually brought her into the heart of history. This age reveals its truth in the form of mass computations produced by those men and women of higher learning who chart and program the process of history. Yet not in classrooms were Dorothy's eyes opened to a revolutionary vision that seized her imagination and fired her spirit, but in the kitchen of her Fifteenth Street apartment.

It had been a curious route by which Peter Maurin had come to her door. He was born in the province of Languedoc, southern France, on May 8, 1869. His parents farmed land that had been in the family for over five centuries, and Peter, with his brothers and sisters who numbered in the teens, lived in the same manner as had the many generations before him. Because his childhood was an experience of community that was based on centuries of family stability, that value was an integral and unalterable part of his person. "I stand on tradition," Peter would say to the young people who gathered around him in the days after he had gotten to know Dorothy.

Still a boy, Peter went to Paris to be educated by the Christian Brothers, a teaching religious order. It was an experience that probably had something to do with his entering the Brothers. But he did not stay, recognizing that his vocation was at least not classroom teaching. What his vocation was apparently remained as unclear to him as it does to many another young person who hears a call but is not certain from where or whom it comes. For a while he was a chocolate salesman on the streets of Paris, an occupation that enabled him to manage his own time, a prime consideration with him throughout his life and one which he regarded as a fundamental attribute of freedom. Concerned with bringing the Catholic Church into political and philosophical harmony with the rising tide of the worldwide movement toward political and social democracy, he joined Marc Sangnier's "Le Sillon" (The Plow), which was dedicated to these objectives. But Maurin seemed to feel that Sangnier's concern was not the ultimate concern of either the Church or the modern world, and further did not like the pamphleteering and demonstrating that went with Sangnier's program.

What Peter did next is not clear, but we know that around the year 1911 he went to Canada in the company of another man in a joint-homesteading venture. When his partner was killed in an accident, he quit the frontier and went south of the border to become an itinerant worker in the American industrial heartland. Years later, Dorothy once asked him what his relationship to the Church had been during these years, and Maurin replied that he had "not lived as a good Catholic should," a statement that Dorothy interpreted to mean that he had been "fooling around" with a woman or women.

Dorothy, of course, did not express herself in these words, as anyone who knew her will readily recognize. She could reach rarefied heights of delicacy when the talk began to tremble around the subject of sex, and in this instance involving Peter her speculative venture was confined to her notes. Even so, she may have been wrong. Peter could well have meant that he had "not lived as a good Catholic should" because he had not used his mind enough.

It certainly seems that the central and almost totally consuming passion of his life was the use of his intellect. That the object of thinking was to *know* was a proposition he accepted in its largest meaning. He would have seen as not only useless, but as time-serving, the notion that speculative ventures should be confined only to areas well supplied with objective data. In his thinking about the meaning and destiny of the person he took account of the entire equation: subject and object, time and eternity. As Dorothy emphasized so many times, he taught a "correlation of the spiritual with the material." In Peter's mind the spiritual was the essential and absolute reality, while the material universe was restless and inchoate, finding its meaning, its beauty, and its order only as it was seen and used by humankind to manifest the truth of the spirit.

Sometimes when he was asked about his social platform he would say, "I am a communitarian." At least on this point, he and Dostoyevsky's Grand Inquisitor agreed. Both saw community as the primal passion which animated life. But the Inquisitor saw this passion as the ultimate source of history's restlessness, for people were forever seeking some sign or principle in which they could be together, which sign or principle was seen as more binding and holy when others were arrayed against it. Their "community" was "good," even godlike, and the "others" were evil.

But Peter saw community as the point of transcendence over time's inchoate restlessness. Community formation began in time, but it did not end in the time-serving formulas of ideologies, class divisions, racial separations, or an inflamed nationalism. Its end was eternity. It was in a direction opposite from the impulses directed toward the possession of power and objects. It was found in the spirit of the Gospels; it was found in giving and not in acquisitiveness. And, said Peter, it was in this redirected view of things, commencing with the subject rather than with the object, that the meaning for life could be rediscovered.

Peter was a true professor in that he professed. His profession was not the consequence of some mystical and private enlightenment, the result of a "hot-line" relationship to Truth. The saccharine platitudes of piety were absent from his vocabulary. His profession was from the mind. He dealt with ideas and continually strove for what he called "clarification"—that is, making the parts fit. He seemed to have lived almost exclusively at the level of ideas. He had always been a reader, and in his wandering years his intellectual quest was so consuming that he became a man of poverty so as to expend his energy in reading and thinking.

At some point, apparently in the mid-twenties, he arrived at what he might have phrased as "the universal solution to the universal problem": what makes the person human and how best the person can fulfill this vision in time. He believed (and for him "belief" was no fevered leap, but the sweet consequences of well-disposed thought) that human destiny was bound to God, and the true work of life was to bring time's lashings into the harmony of eternity. Time should be used to end time.

He believed in conversion. He emphasized it. The term did not, however, mean simply a kind of psychic reversal in which one changed from doubt to belief, followed by a tidying up of one's behavior. Those particular safe-conduct passes to heaven may have been valid, but they were, in a way, a caricature when the rest of humankind, and nature too, were left waiting at the portals. Conversion did mean a change, but it also carried with it the obligation to recognize and resist those depredations on the human spirit that were occurring at the heart of creation and to resist the spirit of "bourgeoisity" and all its works. Conversion meant turning one's vision away from objects toward unity, away from the beguilements of time toward eternity, away from the banal and vulgar toward beauty, and away from the slavery of time's necessities toward freedom. Since all, humankind and nature, were bound into a spiritual unity, it should be the primary concern of those seeking the truth to *know*, to see a creation caught in time's travail in the perspective of eternity.

Peter most assuredly did *not* believe in returning to a formulation of things according to an old design. Designs came from time's necessities, and the face of time was never the same. He more than once emphasized that the objective process had continually to be recast according to an integral humanism that had Christ and the prophets of Israel at its center.

Maurin's revolution went to the heart of the matter, but it was a matter which did not make itself shine with truth and then open itself privately to every person on the basis of a simple exercise of reason. The need for a new creation was one that admitted of no private, relative, or incomplete answers. The answer had to be a community answer, a community bound to the truths of eternity. Only in the Church, Maurin believed, existed the intellectual tradition, the theoretical framework, and the passion for life that took account of the entire equation. The Church did claim to have an integral humanism which infinitely transcended that of any of the time-conceived models of human association. It did carry Christ into time to end time and thereby to end all of time's evil depredations on the person, to end slavery to necessity, to extinguish the spirit of bourgeoisity and make community real, to deny to death its claim of final victory. That the Church had been all too mute in pressing its claims, in shaking loose from a craven dependence on the state and the favored few, was clear to Maurin. "Blowing the Dynamite of the Church" was his quaint way of phrasing his revolutionary expectations where the Church was concerned.

Did the all-encompassing character of Maurin's thought entitle Dorothy to call him a "genius"? That, certainly, must have been a part of it. The passion that lay at the heart of her being would not have allowed her to use that designation for a mind whose range did not reach out for the eternal, for beauty. Though Dorothy was not given to extravagant statement, Peter rang true with her. Every point of his "clarification" seemed to her to be in absolute harmony with the whole. Still, it was not the magnificence and clarity of his mind alone that brought her to use that term. Over the fifteen years of her close association with him she came to see that he *was* what he professed, and she said he was a saint. It was a conviction that remained fixed in her mind from the time of Peter's death until her own.

That he lived outside the conventions of what is regarded as a normal life is obvious. He did not do this for effect; he did it because it simplified his life. The value of the niceties of dress, even of the daily bath, escaped him. His briefcase was the pockets of his coat, into which he stuffed his notes. The same coat, rolled up, not infrequently served as his pillow at night if circumstances decreed that his resting place should be a park bench. He gave his lectures, his "outline of history," to anyone who would listen. He knew Columbia University's Carleton J. Hayes and the Harvard sociologist Pitirim Sorokin, and both, it appears, recognized in Peter something unique to their age, a synthesizing mind which, like the minds of the thinkers of ancient Greece, burned with a desire to understand the place and purpose of the person in the totality of creation. But he was anything but exclusive in whom he sought out to hear his ideas. If any one of the men who sat on the benches in Union Square showed the slightest interest in what Peter was saying, Peter would eagerly press his point.

How curious that he should have found her at all! How he did reads like the poetry of God. He had gone to George Shuster, the editor of *Commonweal,* to talk to him about his ideas, and Shuster had said that Peter should look up Dorothy Day. All Shuster knew was that she lived somewhere near Union Square. So Peter went to Union Square and after several weeks of making inquiries among those forlorn men who sat on benches, he found a "red-headed Irish communist" who knew where Dorothy lived.

It is a medieval tale. The concept fits with Peter because he was a troubadour, singing his idea in public places. Union Square and the area around it would not ordinarily be considered an appropriate place to give a lecture on history. Yet it was there that he was able to find the one student whose mind and spirit were fired by his thought and who saw in his homely dress the shining rags that St. Francis wore.

After his appearance at Dorothy's apartment on that December evening, Peter went there almost daily, to instruct, to explain, and to leave books for her to read. He had her read the Russian philosopher Nikolay Berdyayev, the social thinkers Mikhail Bakunin and Pyotr Kropotkin, histories of the Church, and the lives of the saints. While Dorothy was at times a reluctant student—she was sometimes tired and sometimes, too, she would rather have been doing other things— she came to understand what Peter was talking about. With this understanding came a rising sense of excitement, a revelation of the direction in which her life should go.

But what should she do, Dorothy asked Peter. Begin now, he said. Since she was a journalist, she should start a newspaper to introduce the idea of the personalist revolution to all who would hear it. She should hold "round-table discussions" for the "clarification of thought." Above all, she should feed and clothe the poor.

She began with the newspaper, the *Catholic Worker,* printed by the Paulist Press for fifty-seven dollars. Part of the money she had earned by working for a Paulist priest, Father Joseph McSorley, and the rest came in contributions: ten dollars from a Father Ahearn, the pastor of a Newark inner-city church; and one dollar from Sister Peter Claver Fahy, a Trinitarian nun.

Sister Peter Claver was, and is, a very remarkable woman, a woman of prayer, a vigorous apostle, generous and intelligent. Born in Rome, Georgia, Sister had perhaps an ideal genetic circumstance under which to begin life, an Irish father and a Jewish mother. The dollar that she gave to Dorothy in 1933 not only helped to introduce one of the most unusual pieces of journalism in American history but also inaugurated a significant friendship that lasted throughout Dorothy's lifetime.

So it all began on May 1, 1933. On that day Dorothy and several companions tremulously took their paper into Union Square, where according to the New York *Times* fifty thousand communists were staging a May Day rally. The paper sold for a penny a copy, and neither the price nor the paper ever gave way to bad times or war. What distinguished the paper was Dorothy's "On Pilgrimage" column, which regularly appeared until her death. Her column was personal, but made a point, a clarification of the subject in terms of a spiritual insight.

Almost immediately the *Catholic Worker* became a movement. "Things just happen," Dorothy wrote in the *Catholic Worker*. "Jesus said if your neighbor is hungry, or if your enemy is hungry, feed him. So we took to feeding those who came. . . . The same with sheltering people. The same with starting farms." So the idea took on form and grew, and within a certain perspective it developed an institutional character. But neither Dorothy nor Peter saw the idea as confined to an institutional arrangement. The idea was for all.

3

The Failure of History

In the July-August 1935 issue of the *Catholic Worker,* Dorothy included "The Bourgeois Mind," one of Peter Maurin's short-phrased essays. The ideas he set forth, derived from the Russian thinker Nikolay Berdyayev, represent Maurin's view of the twentieth century and, in his opinion, justified and accentuated the necessity for the personalist revolution. His main point was that what is called the modern age was no longer restrained and directed in its course by a sense of the sacred and that, accordingly, it had opened the way for "the victory of the bourgeois spirit," the spirit of acquisitive individualism. "History has failed," Maurin wrote. "There is no such thing as historical progress; the present is in no wise an improvement on the past. A period of high cultural development is succeeded by another wherein culture deteriorates qualitatively. The will to power, to well being, to wealth, triumphs over the will to holiness, to genius."

However incomprehensible to the modern mind Maurin's analysis of the past three hundred years of history may be, it nonetheless characterizes today's life with considerably more aptness than it did life in 1935. Not only the discord in life in the large actions of history, but the discord at the heart of life, the loss of a sense of well-being in personhood, become with increasing prominence the signs of a stricken time. But then, Maurin's position was not one concocted from whatever inflamed musings might have occurred to him as he sat on the benches of Union Square. His views were largely those of the French personalist thinkers of the pre–World War II period—

Emmanuel Mounier, Jacques Maritain, and Léon Bloy. To these names one must, and always, add the name of Berdyayev, the Russian émigré who after the revolution in his homeland had made Paris his home. "We did depend on Berdyayev," Dorothy once observed.

If the insights of these thinkers are "dated," then truth has no anchor in eternity.

Dorothy Day profoundly believed as Maurin believed. Like him, she was neither liberal nor Marxist because she was not concerned with the management of history's process. Rather she wanted to end that process by seeding into the maelstrom of time the experience of freedom and creativity, by imparting to life a joyous anticipation of the ecstatic point where community was completed and which lay utterly beyond time's ability to mock and desecrate it by death. She was convinced that history's process, whether directed into the channels programmed by liberals or aimed at the Marxist vision of a final beatitude in time, had failed to uphold the humanism for which people had reached throughout time and from the heart of their being. She was not of history; she stood outside of history, and her spirit was vibrant with the passion to end the tyranny of forces that would make contingent and expendable the inviolable uniqueness of personhood.

Maurin's position was the antithesis of the devotion to the idea of progress which has flickered and sometimes glowed through time, but which, in the twentieth century, has become the first article of faith in the world. And so the image of Dorothy confronting history is likely one to produce a chorus of voices, saying: Yes, she was a person of great force and deep spirituality, but what does her spirituality have to do with the forms and character of history's unfolding, especially now, when that unfolding is moving with a new momentum, sweeping the human experience into miraculous vistas that have a glory of their own? And this is a glory for all, for all can see and feel. We do not have to depend upon faith, for to find faith among all of the things that enrapture our senses is hard work and, more frequently than not, a seemingly hopeless struggle.

Still, against the background of this sometimes truculent self-justification, and standing above it, are persons who have seen the crisis into which life is heading. Today, this idea is apparent in the novels of Walker Percy. Just before and after World War I it showed itself with some frequency, notably in William Butler Yeats' "Second Coming," written in 1923. But the three who have dealt with the theme of the crisis in history in terms of how Dorothy understood it and how this crisis gives a particular meaning to her life are Fyodor Dostoyevsky, the Russian novelist; Nikolay Berdyayev, the Russian philosopher of religion and history; and Simone Weil, the French essayist.

One who has known Dorothy, read the *Catholic Worker* or read her two autobiographical books would unquestionably concede that the flashes of truth in Dostoyevsky's perceptions regarding the life of the spirit had laid hold of Dorothy, providing her with insights that have characterized her spirituality. For Dorothy, as perhaps for every person, the critical first question of existence is that of immortality. If there is no immortality, then a life of uninhibited abandonment to the ends of the senses and power is reasonable. Conversely, if the senses and power become exclusively the ends of existence, then there is no real belief in immortality.

In *The Brothers Karamazov* the well-known monologue of the Grand Inquisitor considers immortality in relation to mortality and history. The Inquisitor is the final director of history's process, a figure that has some currency as a literary image. In the scene the Inquisitor lectures a mute and imprisoned Christ on the nature of community. The Inquisitor declares that he knows that the ultimate craving of every person in all of time is for a final and completed unity of all. This quest for community, he says, is "the chief misery of every man individually and of all humanity from the beginning of time." But since death is the destroyer of any hope for a final and completed community, the realization of this hope lies only in a belief in immortality.

But this is a vain hope, the Inquisitor says to Christ. "Thy name" cannot alter time's final depredation of the person, for "beyond the grave" there is nothing. Still, humankind must have its illusions, he continues, but "we shall keep the secret, and for their happiness we shall allure them with the reward of heaven and eternity."

This Inquisitorial judgment denying immortality meant that life had been given over to "the wise and dread spirit, the spirit of self-destruction and non-existence"—Satan. Life then could be lived only in terms of a reconciliation with time. And if time was the all of life, there could be no ecstatic state where community was completed, no final attainment of freedom—in which case, inevitably and finally, "all is permitted."

Nonetheless, this "all is permitted" allowance, of necessity, must be for the social system and not for the individual. Otherwise, blind anarchy would prevail. The Inquisitor *is* the system. He is the manager of history's unfolding; it is he who denies that there is immortality for the individual, yet claims immortality for himself. As he suggests, the individual exists only to serve him. In turn he, out of his calculated humanitarianism, provides people with bread, games, and "innocent dances." For this, humanity will follow him, will "bow down in complete submission" to him. He mocks Christ: had he, Christ, turned the stones into bread, as the devil had ordered him to do, humanity would have enslaved itself to Christ. But Christ had wanted people to affirm him in freedom, not in slavery.

In his last book, *The Possessed,* Dostoyevsky saw the Inquisitorial principle at work in the rising force of atheistic communism. The prophetic elements in this novel are readily discernible in contemporary life and are perhaps more visible in the Western mass-culture nations than in the communist states. One of the arresting prophetic themes in the book is the entrance into life of some new condition that presses toward mediocrity and vulgarization, "wherein culture deteriorates qualitatively," as Maurin said. Especially in the later years of her life Dorothy was deeply disturbed by what she regarded as the increase of the banal, intemperate and raucous elements in the common transactions of daily life. A discussion of the manners of the time would produce a sigh and then her characteristic "Oh, dear." But then she would say, "Beauty will save the world," the substance of which phrase she got from *The Possessed.* Dostoyevsky's point here was that the loss of a transcendent ideal of beauty opened manners, values, and art itself to a corruption by the vulgar and banal. One of the great dramatic scenes in literature is that in which the old professor, giving his final lecture, cries out his ultimate conviction that, before science, before social reform, before technology, the world will be saved by beauty. *The Possessed* was written at a time when the character of life was beginning to be loosed from its traditional moorings and move with an accelerating momentum toward the front line of change. Dostoyevsky recognized that some uncontrollable element had been introduced into history, and he saw it as dehumanizing and potentially fatal.

The Russian thinker Berdyayev, on whom Peter Maurin and Dorothy Day "depended," as Dorothy said, is one of the major interpreters of Dostoyevsky's social and spiritual theorizing, and between Dorothy and Peter on the one hand and Berdyayev on the other there is a considerable identity of thought. Born in 1874 as a member of the nobility, Berdyayev, as a student, became a revolutionary, a position he supported through the Russian revolution of 1917. His experience of this event, however, produced a revolution in his own thinking that led him to Christ, and thereafter his thought was centered on the intellectual and social dispositions of the modern world in relation to the Gospel.

Berdyayev's ideas got their first formal statement in 1919 in a series of lectures he gave in Moscow at the Liberal Academy of Spiritual Culture. The principal theme was that spirit was a reality and that this reality should be the prime factor in ordering history. The point did not ingratiate him with the Bolsheviks, and in 1922 he was expelled from Russia. He lived in Germany until 1926, when he moved to Paris. There, dwelling in the suburb of Clamart, with his wife, his sister-in-law, and his cat (the latter as cherished as any member of the household), he lived out his years, dying in 1949.

In his *The Meaning of History*, first published in 1936, Berdyayev stated his conviction that "There can be little doubt that not only Russia but Europe and the world as a whole are now entering upon a catastrophic period in their development. . . . Volcanic sources have opened in the historical substrata. Everything is tottering." World War II, of course, did nothing but reinforce this conviction with him. In his last years he wrote his autobiographical *Dream and Reality*, an account of the further development of his philosophical and religious ideas. In the concluding chapter, "Final Philosophical Outlook," he predicted the end of the modern world. "A terrible judgment hangs over history and civilization," he wrote. "History shows constant signs of a fatal lapse from the human or divine-human to the sub-human or demonic. Out of this idolatrous and demonolatrous instinct man conjures up real demonic powers which in turn seize control of him." History was undergoing an "internal cataclysm."

What did he mean by this phrase, "internal cataclysm?" He meant that a vision of a Christian humanism was becoming obliterated. Within time, within the natural process of history, ungoverned by any overriding idea that would focus the human impulse to a point above that process, there could be nothing but an enslavement of the person to the necessities of process. When that occurred, there could be no reach for beauty.

This "internal cataclysm" was not a gradual wearing away of old forms supplanted by new. Berdyayev saw the change occurring in an accelerating, outward expansion of the technical, cultural systems from which people had once erected a meaning for life but which now had become itself the source of that meaning. He called this change "objectification" because it was what occurred when the "objective," exclusive of the spiritual dimension, became the sole measure of reality. Inevitably, this objectified knowing, building on an ever-enlarging base of past knowledge, made its way from the individual toward the general, toward larger and larger systems which were increasingly complicated and increasingly tenuous, and with an ever-mounting necessity for adjustment.

The consequences of this "progress," especially since World War II, have become, as Berdyayev saw, inhibitors of personal creativity. The reason underlying this truth is simple: an increase in the number of objects in which life is involved produces an increase in the complexity of the system that is necessary to keep them in a working harmony. Since the supply of objects and of data is inexhaustible, the system takes on an accelerating complexity.

In his "Final Philosophical Outlook," Berdyayev took an image from the Book of Revelations to give character to the potential of the system to destroy true creativity, which of itself is a spiritual dimension of life. The image from Revelations is that of "the beast rising out of the sea." The "beast," in scriptural usage, is the dread sign of a final and cataclysmic time. He is the destroyer of the Church, a parody of the risen Christ, and the soul of the principle of the total system. His animating spirit is not directed toward community but toward the totality of the "I." There is no "we" in his reference. His quest is for power, not service; for objects, not beauty.

It was the "system" that nourished this spirit, because service to the system frequently meant a nullification of personal creativity.

The system demanded an allegiance to its own perpetuation, and whatever unique endowment for creativity a person might possess, to add to life the richness and beauty of his or her own special gift, was "decreated" so that service to the system could be complete.

The spirit of bourgeoisity, by finding its outlet in the creation of systems, turned one of the sources of the joy of life into darkness, for the creative act was a source of joy. Romain Rolland, a French writer of the early twentieth century and Nobel Prize winner, in his story "Lightning Strikes Christophe," makes creativity and joy synonymous: "Joy, and furious joy, the sun lights up all that is and will be, the godlike joy of creation! There is no joy but in creation. There are no living beings but those who create. All the rest are shadows, hovering over the earth, strangers to the light."

The rising beast of Revelations, the spirit of bourgeoisity, signaled the end of history, the final sign before Christ's Second Coming. Convinced of this, Berdyayev felt as the early Christians had felt at the height of their persecution by Nero. Christ had said that he would come again, and soon. What did two thousand years mean in the face of that promise? Time, to Berdyayev, was the "evil nightmare," and with Christ there was no time.

Berdyayev's hope for the Second Coming was not one of waiting for the cataclysmic fireworks that are presumably to go off when the end is near; when the number "666" is blazoned across the sky; when the "saved" are swept out of it all, leaving the rest to fry, the earth all ablaze. "It may be possible," he writes, "to await passively the judgment of a revengeful deity, but no such attitude is compatible with the Second Coming. . . . This event will be a transition from historical Christianity, which foreshadows the end of the spell-bound world of ours." It would be an event characterized, not by "fear, inertia and frustration, but one of daring and creative endeavor. Historical Christianity has grown cold and intolerably prosaic; its activity consists mainly of adapting itself to the commonplace, to the bourgeois patterns and habits of life."

When Christ came again it would be to ignite a heavenly fire on earth. "That fire will not be kindled until the fire of man is set ablaze." It would not be the fire that burned in those revolutionary causes which promised to bring immediately the perfect society that time had promised. It would be the fire that had eternity as its vision

—the point where community would be completed and final. It would be a fire ignited by "every moral act of life, of mercy and of sacrifice" and "would bring to pass the end of the world where hatred, cruelty and selfishness reign supreme"—a fire that would be seen in "every creative act directed against the kingdom of necessity, servitude and inertia" and would "bring with it the promise of a new and 'other' world where God's power is revealed in freedom and love."

These qualities, which according to Berdyayev would show the light of one "ablaze" with the fire of heaven, surely describe Dorothy, for if anyone has looked from the darkness of despair to heaven's light it was she. And if anyone has struggled, day after day, to tell of the beauty of that light to all who would listen, it was she.

Simone Weil was another person ablaze with the heavenly fire, one willing to be consumed by it all for the beauty of that light. She was a Parisian, contemporary to Maritain and Berdyayev, but not of their company. Like them, she had a brilliant and prophetic mind, but her course and experience were singularly her own. There is something deeply appealing about this young Jewess, her innocence, her awkwardness, her purity, and with this, a feeling of concern for her bouts of intense physical suffering. Her ideas and insights have been frequently analyzed and discussed, and she herself has undergone a measure of scrutiny, for she was altogether extraordinary. But psychological form-fitting explains little and diminishes nothing in a mind that moved so directly and piercingly toward truth.

Simone Weil did not know of Dorothy Day; yet, in a direct and almost prophetic way, no person points more directly to the significance of Dorothy's spirituality than does Simone Weil. Born in Paris in 1906, she did graduate work in philosophy and later tried teaching, although she was not very successful at it. In her graduate school days she was a Marxist, but during the thirties, as a result of several intense mystical experiences, she turned wholly to the person of Christ for a meaning for existence, and it was to this idea that she gave the highest use of her life.

Although Weil does not mention Berdyayev in her essays, there are some close similarities between her thought and his, and one theme that they held in common was the failure of history. Like Berdyayev, she thought that something alien had begun to work in life. In one of her essays, "The Love of God and Affliction," she says that "we are living in times that have no precedent, and in our present situation universality, which could formerly be implicit, has to be fully explicit." This statement carries a meaning similar to Berdyayev's "objectification." It means that humankind, which once had seen all things in terms of the design of heaven, had turned to objects in an expectation of human fulfillment. In so doing, humanity had "turned its gaze away from God and walked in the wrong direction." For a while after that a person could at least walk. But now "we are nailed down to the spot, only free to choose which way we look, ruled by necessity. A blind mechanism, heedless of degrees of spiritual perfection, continually tosses men about and throws some of them at the very foot of the Cross. It rests with them to keep or not to keep their eyes turned toward God through all the jolting. It does not mean that God's Providence is lacking. It is in his Providence that God has willed that necessity should be like a blind mechanism."

This "blind mechanism," this movement toward the exclusively objective, produced what Weil called "affliction." She meant by this term the rootless, spirit-bereft character of lives that were ordered to the necessities of a technological culture, where the spirit of bourgeoisity at every point demanded subservience to its values. "Affliction is anonymous before all things; it deprives its victims of their personality and makes them into things. It is indifference; and it is the coldness of this indifference—a metallic coldness—that freezes all those it touches right to the depths of their souls. . . . They will never believe anymore that they are anyone."

The most terrible part of affliction, she continued, was that it "makes God appear to be absent for a time, more absent than a dead man, more absent than light in the utter darkness of a cell. A kind of horror submerges the whole soul. During this absence there is nothing to love, the soul ceases to love. God's absence becomes final." And what remains for the soul, so finally afflicted? It "has to go on loving the emptiness, or at least to go on wanting to love, though it may only be with an infinitesimal part of itself. Then one day God will come to show himself to this soul and to reveal the beauty of the world to it, as in the case of Job. But if the soul stops loving it falls, even in this life, into something almost equivalent to hell."

In her essay "Last Thoughts," Weil said that what the world
needed was a new kind of saint. "Today it is not merely enough to be
a saint . . . we must have the saintliness demanded by the present
moment, a new saintliness, itself also without precedent." She knew,
she said, that her countryman, Maritain, had been saying the same
thing. He had, however, "only enumerated the aspects of saintliness
of former days, which for the time being at least, have become out of
date."

But a "new type of sanctity is indeed a fresh spring, an invention.
. . . It is almost equivalent to a new revelation of the universe and
of human destiny. It is the exposure of a large portion of truth and
beauty hitherto concealed under a thick layer of dust. More genius
was needed than was needed by Archimedes to invent mechanics and
physics." A new saintliness, sufficient to the crisis at hand, would be
"a still more marvelous invention." Then she urged that "God's
friends pray in Christ's name for saints who possessed genius, for the
world needs saints who have genius, just as a plague-stricken town
needs doctors."

Simone Weil's "new" saint was one whose spirituality was a
sword, penetrating to the malign source of elements that had brought
history's process into crisis. This new saint would openly and ac-
tively confront those conditions of life that made it appear that God
was absent and that the soul had ceased to love. Perhaps Dorothy
was this "marvelous invention."

One is inclined to believe that Simone Weil, too, was herself the
saint-genius that she wanted to see in the world. Perhaps she was, for
she placed all of the resources of her marvelous mind and her meager
physical stamina at the service of God. Under the title *Waiting for
God*, G. P. Putnam's Sons in 1951 published her letters and essays.
They reveal insights and points of emphasis which repeatedly be-
speak an affinity with Dorothy's positions. How completely, for example, does the following statement represent a conviction held by
Dorothy: "The children of God should not have any other country
here below but the universe itself, with the totality of all the reason-
ing creatures it ever has contained, contains, or ever will contain.
This is the native city to which we owe our love."

Or: "Every existing thing is equally upheld in its existence by

God's creative love. The friends of God should love him to the point of merging their love into his with regard to all things here below."

Or this question: "How can Christianity call itself catholic if the universe itself is left out?"

And how Dorothy would have been struck by this phrase: "Beauty is eternity here below."

Simone Weil, the servant of God who spoke so profoundly of God's seeming absence from life, was never baptized. Dorothy read Simone Weil and undoubtedly believed that she had been baptized by her desire for truth and beauty. And that she was a Jew was a special anointment always regarded by Dorothy as a sign of a close kinship with God.

4

Fathers Hugo and Lacouture

On that December day in 1927, when Dorothy took the ferry to Staten Island to be baptized, no cherubs who may have been flying around in New York's harbor touched her spirit with attar or made it glow with light. Her mood was one of an almost grim determination to do what she had set out to do. But gradually, by working persistently and conscientiously in the practice of her faith, and by studying the history and mind of the Church, she experienced a growing awareness of what she was about that was like an anointment. No holy card was ever so laden with treacle but what she could not find substance in it, or any rite performed so perfunctorily but what she felt the good of it. Then, after five years of this, Peter Maurin began to teach her and brought her as a Catholic into a confrontation with what he saw as the perverse tendencies of history where the Christian ends of life were concerned.

Was this enough for Dorothy, that she had found a vocation, a place in the Church? It was not. It should be said repeatedly that she was a person with an incomparable passion for what she called "the hard contest." That the battle she chose to enter was against those seemingly inviolable canons which now govern the character of history's unfolding might suggest that she was deluded. She was not. She was David; and the world, whose systems and values were producing portents of its own death, was her Goliath. Like David she breathed the air of invincibility because she knew her strength. Her armament was the weapons of the spirit, and to arm herself for "the hard contest," as she phrased it, was the profoundest impulse of her being. She seemed always to be famished for spiritual food.

It was, of course, that watchful and perceptive sentinel, Sister Peter Claver, who opened the way for Dorothy to avail herself of the spiritual weapons she sought. In five pages of notes which Sister made on August 20, 1985, she recalls the circumstances that introduced Dorothy to the spiritual retreat which, in Sister's words, "made Dorothy holy."

In the late thirties, Sister notes, she was stationed with the Catholic Charities at Mobile, Alabama. In her work there, she came into contact with a Father Frank Giri, "a prayerful and extremely zealous priest." During this period Father Giri saw an announcement in the *Ecclesiastic Review* that a Jesuit priest, Father Onesimus Lacouture from Canada, would give an eight-day retreat for priests during which the retreatants would observe complete silence. So Father Giri went to Baltimore to make the retreat. When he returned to Mobile he was "filled with joy and enthusiasm" because he had gotten a glimpse of the "true radical Gospel teachings." Father Giri, Sister notes, "immediately sought me out to share with me his experience. After telling me about it, the eagerness and acceptance of the priests who made it, he gave me a brief copy of notes . . . taken by Fr. Egan of Baltimore. Fr. Egan died of a brain tumor shortly after the retreat. When Fr. Giri gave me the notes he told me to use them for meditation only before the Blessed Sacrament."

Shortly after this, Sister was missioned to Gillette, New Jersey, where she was to renovate an old farmhouse which had been given to her community, the Missionary Servants of the Most Blessed Trinity. The place had not been inhabited for twenty-five years and, in the meantime, the area around it had become suburban. The renovation was aimed at making the old home into a retreat center. Toward this end the community treasurer gave Sister a hundred dollars with which to install indoor plumbing but which only got the water pipes laid up to the house.

Then Dorothy heard of Sister's dilemma and suggested to some men in the breadline at the Catholic Worker house on Mott Street that they go and help her. "Chris carved a crucifix for the Chapel. People came in mysterious ways to help . . . to turn a broken-down farm house into a quiet, beautiful retreat house for the poor."

In the course of the work, "Dorothy came to Gillette for a day of quiet and prayer. Being filled with Father Lacouture's teaching, I gave her the notes Fr. Giri had given me and suggested she go to our retreat house in Stirling which was up a winding hill from Gillette overlooking a peaceful beautiful Jersey valley. The spot would be quieter, more restful. I instructed her, as Fr. Giri had instructed me, to use the notes . . . before the Blessed Sacrament. In the late afternoon, when she returned to Gillette, she asked me, 'where can I find priests who are giving this retreat?' I told her the retreats were being given by Fr. John Hugo and Fr. Louis Farina at an orphanage at Oakmont, Pa., that Fr. Farina was the chaplain there. Oakmont was on the outskirts of Pittsburgh."

Since Dorothy dated her retreat notes only when she felt in a formal mood, one cannot be certain when she went to Oakmont for the first time. Sister Peter Claver says that it was in 1939 and Father Hugo thought it was in 1940. In any case, the atmosphere that she describes while riding the bus to Oakmont suggests the opening of World War II. This bus ride presents an image on which to reflect: the armies of Europe, with all of their new technological paraphernalia, posturing to launch their terror onto the world while this woman, a warrior of the spirit, rode alone to have eight days of silence.

On her return to New York, Sister continues, Dorothy "phoned me and spoke with joy that she had found a community faith and a gospel spirituality she termed . . . 'the bread of the strong.' " Days later, Sister went to visit Dorothy at Mott Street and then, as the afternoon began to grow late, "we walked across lower Manhattan together where I was to get the Hudson Tubes back to New Jersey. We sat on a park bench under the shadow of the tower of the Tombs, New York City's largest prison. We talked, we were loath to part. Dorothy said on this occasion, 'at last I have found what I was looking for when I left my communist friends and became a Catholic.' "

Where Dorothy's spiritual thirst was concerned, Sister was then and would be a cistern that was always filled with good water.

This retreat became one of the principal sources of Dorothy's spiritual energy for the remainder of her life. She took it many times during the years after 1940, and most often as directed by Father

Hugo. There were, however, other retreat directors over the course of the next decade of whom Dorothy speaks in her notes as having served her well: Louis Farina and Joseph Meenan of Pittsburgh; Marion Casey of St. Paul; Denis Mooney, Franciscan; and John Osterreicher of Seton Hall College. Another priest whose retreats made their mark on Dorothy and about whom she writes in *The Long Loneliness* was Father Pacifique Roy, a Josephite.

The last retreat that Dorothy attended was that given by Father Hugo in July 1975. As she left the retreat center and was telling Father goodbye, she asked him to give the homily at her funeral. As matters turned out, he could not fulfill her request. But what did it matter? His contribution to Dorothy's life, as a retreat director, as a counselor and friend, had been made. For over a period of forty years he had given her the best he could from his priestly vocation, and at the time of his own death he seemed to feel that, with all the tumult and the dry times he had experienced over the years, he had kept the faith and had provided Dorothy with the spiritual food that had made her holy.

On August 1, 1981, Father gave his sister, Cecilia Marie Hugo, a brief biography to be used at the time of his death. It is a sparse chronology of parishes served, concluding with his appointment in 1970 as the resident chaplain for the Sisters of the Holy Family of Nazareth at their Provincial House, Mt. Nazareth, in northern Pittsburgh. His chronology concludes with the statement that "in 1976 Dorothy Day, who had done so much to foster the growth of the original series of retreats, came again to make a retreat with some of her friends, thus initiating a new series that has continued ever since." All that remained for his sister to add was the date of his death. He realized that his mortal end was not far off, for he had a bad heart. But death came on October 1, 1985, from a car accident. He was seventy-four years old, forty-nine of which had been in the priesthood.

Ordained on June 14, 1936, Father Hugo had scholarly interests and abilities as a speaker which suggested a teaching role as the proper course for his vocational work. Six years in academic life apparently convinced him it was not what he wanted. Beginning in 1942, and for a decade thereafter, he served as an assistant in several parishes. After five years as a prison chaplain at the Allegheny

County Workhouse and Jail, he became the founding pastor of a newly established parish in a Pittsburgh suburb. There he served for ten years, then took leave to prepare some theological reports for Bishop John Wright. After this and several other special assignments, he was given what turned out to be his last work, his chaplaincy at the Mt. Nazareth Center.

This account, taken from Father Hugo's chronology, sounds as if his priestly life had run an inauspicious course. But beneath this recital of a routine career there had been storms, and he had preferred that they not be mentioned. The trouble, perhaps, was that at the core of his being were a rigor and a thirst for certitude that did not admit of taking the comfortable and popular way. In his *Deliverance of Onesimus,* a book which he himself published shortly before his death, he occasionally reveals the sharp edge of his view on certain dispositions in the priestly life. In one instance he speaks of "hyphenated priests," by which he meant, "those priests who so readily relinquish the primary source of power to hobble along on crutches." Among the hobblers, as he saw it, was a type sometimes found in Catholic educational institutions, the "priest-academic . . . soul-mates of those scribes to whom we hear Jesus refer stingingly . . . those who 'seeing do not see and hearing do not understand.' "

Continuing, Father Hugo enlarges on the theme of the incomplete priest. All priests, he says, "know that they should change lives—this belongs to their calling—and they are frustrated when they cannot. . . . Although priests, they are loath to pay the price demanded by God for spiritual efficacy—which is to become saints."

Of course Father Hugo might have made his point in somewhat more rarefied and roundabout terms, but he did not have a gift for dissimulation. Still, as a young priest-academic himself in the mid-thirties, he found himself in the class of those priests whom he later would see as incompletely formed and whom he would call upon to become whole. It was only "in the nick of time" that he came to a new and radical conception of his priestly character. He had gone, with some of his brother priests, to a retreat given by Father Lacouture. This retreat, given in Baltimore, was presumably the one that Father Giri had attended and which had prompted his exultant report to Sister Peter Claver. As for Father Hugo, it was "then and there" that he began "to articulate an intent . . . to spend the rest of my days as a priest diffusing the magnificent vision of the Christian life that I had been contemplating during those glorious eight days at the seminary in Baltimore."

This was the origin of what Dorothy called "the famous retreat" which had such a profound effect on her own life. She was never able to take the retreat directly from Father Lacouture, but she studied him, corresponded with him, and paid high tribute to him in her writings. For her, this gentle and humble person opened a radical spirituality that fired her being and lifted her to heights that she had never dreamed of reaching.

In *The Deliverance of Onesimus,* Father Hugo gives a brief biography of Father Lacouture. Onesimus (named after a slave converted by St. Paul) was born on April 13, 1881, on a farm in Quebec province, Canada. The elder Lacouture married twice and altogether fathered twenty-one children, of whom Onesimus was nineteenth.

When Onesimus was six the family moved to the United States, eventually settling in Cochituate, Massachusetts. There he learned English and went to high school, where he took the classical course. When he was seventeen he decided to become a priest, and, caught up in a passion for the glory of knowledge, he decided to enter the Society of Jesus.

The life of books and fraternal discourse escaped him. When the time came for him to go out and teach, as Jesuits do before ordination, he was sent to the wilds of the Yukon to catechize the Eskimos. At first, he found it almost unbearably lonely, and he began to wonder at the strange course that his vocation was taking. Gradually, though, the beauty of the northland and the goodness in the lives of the people that he had come to instruct began to moderate his feelings. His pleasure came in taking long walks.

It was on these walks, Father Hugo says, that Onesimus achieved an insight that appeared to be one of the principal positions on which he built his spirituality. Its complete accord with the Creator's design gave nature its beauty. The river flowed as it must; the clouds moved as they were directed; and the wolf ate its prey only to sustain his position in the order of things. But in humankind there was an urge for an unbounded dominion over nature—even to ravage it—so as to serve that impulse which drives people to possess power and objects. Onesimus knew nothing of Berdyayev, but Berdyayev would have known what Onesimus, in the wilds of the North, had come to recognize. It was that "the spirit of bourgeoisity" could destroy beauty.

Then, back in the compound, continues Father Hugo, Onesimus found the sustaining strength to take with a good spirit the discipline and directives of his supervisor by reading St. John of the Cross. There he found these words: "Every man naturally desireth to know, but what availeth knowledge without the fear of God? A meek husbandman that serveth God is more acceptable to Him than a curious philosopher who, considering the course of heaven, wilfully forgetteth himself. . . . Let us therefore cease from the desire of such vain knowledge, for oft times is found therein great distraction and deceit of the enemy, whereby the soul is much hindered and withheld from the perfect and true love of God."

To be sure, some criticisms of the retreats were made from that high level where the perfect order of doctrinal purity is understood, and it was said that Father Lacouture had not understood that order. He had placed nature in opposition to grace and therefore had placed a black spot on God's perfection. But this charge, says Father Hugo, was untrue, as untrue as the charges brought against St. John of the Cross, Father Lacouture's teacher. St. John had even been assaulted by his Carmelite brethren and then cited before the Inquisition. But the falsity of the charges against him was finally proclaimed by the Church, which canonized St. John and then declared him a Doctor of the Church. Father Lacouture had not placed nature in opposition to grace; he had made nature the model from which ascended the path to heaven.

Father Hugo himself made two retreats under Father Lacouture in the summer of 1939, just before Father Lacouture was silenced. What was there about these retreats that touched Father Hugo as deeply vital? It certainly came from no dynamic posturing on the part of the man himself. As Father Hugo relates, Father Lacouture was no orator or "tub-thumper." He spoke a simple language which sometimes flashed with wit. "He had no distinctive doctrinal teaching of his own, no innovations other than fresh ways of presenting basic Christian teaching, no abstruse theological speculations, no novelties. . . ."

At the heart of the retreat there was, in Father Hugo's words, a "radical Christianity." Continuing this thought, Father Hugo added that "a true disciple cannot escape the cruciform pattern of Christian living." Scripture could be quoted at length to support this position, and Father Hugo quotes Scripture: "Behold I send you as lambs in the midst of wolves." "Blessed are you when men hate you, and when they exclude and revile you, on account of the Son of man." "Woe to you, when all men speak well of you, for so did their fathers to the false prophets."

In particular instances of slight or hurt, these quotations may be useful to cool the fever of the wound, but in the sense of the Lacouture retreat they implied a reversal of the flow patterns into which life, often casually and uncritically, usually falls. It meant turning away from Berdyayev's "bourgeoisity" toward community, where the "I" loses all of its individualistic character to become "we." It meant turning away from the enticements of the object toward the needs of the person, especially with respect to the need for creativity; it meant turning from war to peace, and from a culture that was debauched and strident to one of harmony—the harmony that came from an ideal of beauty.

The retreat was evangelical, in the sense that an emphasis was placed not on a contemplation of the sinfulness and unworthiness of the person, but on the person's destiny "in love" to share in the glory of God's kingdom. The controversial character of the retreat obviously arose largely from its emphasis on the spirituality of St. John of the Cross, his insistence on "detachment" from those impulses for power and possessions to which the person was subject. In his *The Ascent to Mount Carmel,* this sixteenth-century Carmelite, "renowned for his holiness and extraordinary sweetness of nature," counseled those who sought God to "always prefer 'not the thing which is easiest but that which is hardest, not the most pleasant but that which is least pleasant . . . desiring to be stripped and emptied of everything the world can offer and to be poor for Christ's sake,' promising the soul which pursued this course great consolation. . . ."

The "great consolation" of which the saint spoke was an increased knowledge of living in the light of God's love. What did "creatures" matter when compared to the glory of that light? For love was transcending, liberating, the final all-sufficient and eternal reality. This exaltation of the power of love was one of the continuing principles of the retreat. The other, existing in the harmony of a complete and inseparable unity with love, was what St. Paul called "the folly of the cross," the phrase that comes from the paschal mystery of Christ's death and resurrection.

A mystery indeed!—so boundless in its reach that all of creation was subject to its work, so joy-filled with meaning, so totally a declaration of love, that it could only have come from the mind and spirit of a God—the God! It was the mystery of the cosmic drama of good and evil, of time and eternity, of Satan and Truth. It was the substance of the drama of creation that, when it arose out of the void, it bore with it, from the fires beneath, the Satanic curse of time—that all that came out of time would die—that the struggling process of nature would have no end—firmaments would blaze anew but become black holes in the end—and that men and women, with all their dreams, their reach for beauty, and their joy in the work of creation, would, in time, return to the void, where even those mystic chords of love that bound one to another, and to all, would seem to have no destiny but nothingness.

The exaction of time was certain and it was absolutely implacable, for the dying began even as life began. There was also suffering, for out of that cauldron underlying the good of creation arose a negation, making its way through the imperfections and crevasses of life to afflict whomever it might. The wanton randomness of its action was a sign of its evil source, for the blameless suffered, too, and there was no sign in time more striking in its poignancy than that of suffering innocence. The glory of Easter was the paschal lamb, the Lamb of God, descending into the cauldron, taking there the light of eternity, and leaving it there as a sign that in the end that light would banish death and remove every shadow of suffering from all who had ever lived, whether suffering of tortures, purges, and annihilations, of agony and death from cancer, of all those unspeakable diseases that could pinion a person to a final, pain-racked descent into the grave. And the mystery was that all would live forever in the light of glory.

The Lacouture retreat thus ascended to epic proportions, and it was done in a way that moved many to see the revolutionary and blinding light of the mystery that was at the heart of life.

When Father Lacouture was silenced, Father Hugo began himself to give a retreat on the Lacouture model. At his retreat at Oakmont, at the beginning of World War II, Dorothy began her ascent to a new level of life.

In the December 1951 issue of the *Catholic Worker,* Dorothy set down what the retreat had meant for her:

> What was it that we were so taken with in the retreat? Of course it was stimulating, glowing, alive, challenging. . . . [N]one of us laymen made it under Fr. Lacouture, but most of the retreat masters we heard were good teachers.
>
> For too long, too little has been expected of us. When Christ spoke, He spoke from the Mount to the multitudes. He called on all men to take up their cross and follow Him. When we listened to Fr. Lacouture's retreat, we began to understand the distinction between nature and the supernatural . . . and saw for the first time the incomparable heights to which man is called. We saw for the first time man's spiritual capacities, raised as he is to be a child of God. We saw the basis of our dignity.
>
> I could write a great deal about that retreat, and all it brought to us, the new vistas which opened out before us. But I will simply say that it gave us spiritual direction. We were learning how to die to ourselves, to live in Christ, and all the turmoil of the movement, all the pruning of natural love, all the disappointment were explained by the doctrine of the Cross, in the folly of the Cross. The retreat gave us hope and courage, as retreats were supposed to do, and we will be everlastingly grateful for it, grateful to Fr. Lacouture, who made the retreat possible for us. We feel that we have been participants of a great spiritual movement which is still going on, though it is perhaps now in shadow. The seed has fallen into the ground and died. But we know that it will bear fruit.

For the next thirty years she carried out the work that began on May Day, 1933. With those others who, struck by her vision, had come to join her life and to sustain her, she fed the poor and tried to comfort those who came to be nourished in spirit as well as in body. During the last fifteen years of her life she suffered from a failing heart, and this increasingly took her strength and heightened her vulnerability to the rising crescendo of discord which was arising from the world and which, at times, seemed to reverberate within her own flesh.

"In the evening of life we shall be judged on love," wrote St. John of the Cross. In this era when even the word "love" means something that has lost all harmony with an ideal of beauty and of the eternal, Dorothy has lived for love and suffered for love in a way that is a striking example of how beauty can be restored. When Dostoyevsky's doddering old professor says that "beauty will save the world," he is referring to the beauty that is built on love.

Three weeks before Dorothy's death, Sister Peter Claver, moved by a sudden impulse, had gone from Baltimore to Maryhouse, the Catholic Worker house of hospitality in New York. Making her way up several flights of stairs, she entered Dorothy's room to find her seated in a shadowed and recessed part of the room. Dorothy herself was almost a shadow, but she greeted Sister with delight. Seating herself, Sister handed Dorothy a transcript of the conferences which Father Hugo had used in giving the retreat and which he had asked Sister to give to Dorothy. She took it and clasped it to her, and then, reaching out to touch a flower in a vase on the table, she said, "I am still sowing."

Part Two

ALL IS GRACE

All of the reflections in this section are Dorothy Day's, and unless otherwise noted are taken from her manuscript "All Is Grace." Liberty has occasionally been taken in reconstructing some of her material, for to read it is sometimes to wrestle with abbreviations, ellipses, and approximate quotations whose source may be obscure. Coherence, too, can be elusive, and it is not always clear who is talking— Dorothy, the retreat director, or some saint of past times. So, in order to make understandable what she is saying, I have at times translated her shorthand into words and infused her text with interpolations so as to make her meaning clear. Brackets confine interpolations.

Whose ideas are being given is another matter. The substance of the retreat is traditional retreat material, but given a distinctive internal emphasis by the retreat masters. It was what Dorothy saw as the piercing truth of these emphases that made the retreats so vital to her. She *did* truly "see." All things *did* become "new" for her. The reason for the retreat's effectiveness was that she had, as she often said, good teachers. It was Father Lacouture who built the structure of the retreat, which structure after 1939 was taken over by Father Hugo. So these two priests, as well as the several others who gave the retreat, are also in a sense the authors of Dorothy's work. But there need be no concern over the possible prospect of an absence of Dorothy from the text. She is decidedly there, giving it the force of her own discovery, her own intensity, and the light of her vast reading.

"God bless Dorothy!" one might exclaim. God bless her because

she read and she wrote—gifts from her father through inheritance
and by precept. God bless her because she read out of her "field,"
and because her writing was alight with an almost unparalleled store
of knowledge that came from her reading. And, it can be added, God
obviously did bless her—especially with a mind that could bring all
of this knowledge into the light of the grace which had changed her
life and which could order it to the truths that she got from the
retreats.

In addition to the "All Is Grace" manuscript, other sources used
are Dorothy's "Notebook," "notes," fragments, and selected letters
that were among the material she gave me in 1975. When these are
used they are noted.

1

The Early Retreats

DOROTHY'S INTENTION IN WRITING THE RETREAT NOTES

What I wanted to do was just to give a taste of a retreat as though to say—"Come and see that the Lord is sweet. Learn of Him and find rest for your souls. . . ." I wrote at length on some aspects of the retreat, more briefly on others. I started making them [her retreat reflections] as clear as I could for a friend [her sister, Della] . . . so I could pass them on to her as a letter, a very long one which she could read at her leisure.

AN EARLY RETREAT

This account is taken from the original manuscript. A variant of it is published in Dorothy's *The Long Loneliness* (Image Books, 1959).

In the city there is the convent of Mary Reparatrix on 28th Street, just across from The Little Church Around the Corner with its fashionable weddings. Convent, Retreathouse and Church were all enclosed by high buildings and there was no garden such as the Cenacle to walk in, and the first time I made what is termed a private retreat there, alone by myself, visited by one of the cloistered nuns between my interminable periods of solitude, left to read retreats of by-gone days which aimed to make you begin a retreat in a state of remorse, self examination, penitence—I endured it for two days and could not wait to get away, to get out on the streets where I could breathe, walk freely, sense my freedom from restraint. I felt that I had been in jail, in solitary confinement. Probably I was suffering from what I later came to term the spiritual "bends." The atmosphere was too rarified for me. "Man is not made to live alone," I consoled myself for my failure. "If I had been with a group, I would have been happy. I would have enjoyed it." Some-how I always associated joy and happiness with the religious life.

THE CATHOLIC WORKER COMMUNITY RETREAT

Dorothy was at pains from the first to emphasize and clarify the spiritual center of the work in which she and her young associates were engaged. In 1936 she and her friends got possession of an old farm just out of Easton, Pennsylvania, where they hoped to put into effect Peter Maurin's agrarian emphasis on social re-creation. An itinerant Josephite priest, Father Pacifique Roy, who had taken the Lacouture retreat, took up residence at the farm and began to give retreats for the community there. Dorothy found them so spiritually edifying that she began to think of the retreat as a necessary and continuing center for the life of the community. In September 1939 she wrote this editorial for the *Catholic Worker:*

> Again and again Christ had to get away from the multi-tudes who were thronging about Him to be healed, to be fed, and to hear His words. We read of how He went away into desert places to pray. He went out in a boat. He stopped to rest by the well. He went up on a mountain. He even had to get away from His chosen friends. . . . Last month, seventy-two of our fellow workers came together at

Easton . . . withdrawing themselves for a time from the work to pray. . . . The retreat was given by Fr. Joachim Benson, editor of the Preservation of the Faith, a member of the order of the Missionary Servants of the Most Holy Trinity. . . . For three days we had a closed retreat, silence was kept, as much as was humanly possible, no problems were discussed, no reading was done which was not spiritual. It was a time of real happiness.

For the past few years we have had colloquiums and when they were over, and the hours of discussion were past, everyone left, glad to get away from each other, glad to be free of all the talk. Problems did not seem to get settled. By the time this retreat was over, and we gathered together for a social evening of talk and discussion, we found such unity amongst us all, that there seemed no reason for discussion. When we separated, it was with pain, we hated to leave each other, we loved each other more truly than ever before, and felt that sense of comradeship, that sense of Christian solidarity which will strengthen us for the work. Living as we do in the midst of thousands, almost in the streets, I am often reminded of our quest:

I will arise and go about the city; in the streets and broad ways I will seek Him whom my soul loveth.

I sought Him and I found Him not. . . . But, when I had a little passed by them, I found Him whom my soul loveth: I held Him and I will not let Him go.

[The Song of Songs]

THE FIRST OF THE FATHER JOHN HUGO RETREATS

In a folder containing material on these retreats, Dorothy wrote: "These retreats went on from Labor Day 1940, I believe, thru the War years at Maryfarm, Easton, Pennsylvania and up to 1949 at Maryfarm, Newburgh, N.Y. with Jane O'Donnell (The Grail, Philadelphia, Pa.) and other young women in charge." In a letter dated July 22, 1941, Dorothy summoned her fellow workers to a retreat.

She began by informing them that the retreat would be at the Worker farm at Easton, Pennsylvania, was to begin on the evening of August 26, and would run for a week. The retreat master was to be Father John J. Hugo of Pittsburgh. Dorothy continues:

> We do not need to insist on its importance. We all realize that no excuse, 'we have taken a wife,'—'we have bought a farm'—'we have a new yoke of oxen' is a valid one for CW's. It is just because of the importance of the work that we must drop everything and spend one week listening to the Lord, who will speak only if we keep silence.
>
> It is no use worrying about what will happen to the houses, the farms, in our absence. If we depend on our own efforts, we are deluding ourselves. What we are aiming at is to bring men back to Christ, and it is presumption and effrontery and arrogance, if we try to do it without looking after ourselves first. . . . Here is a time offered, to renew ourselves, to taste and see, that the Lord is sweet. . . .
>
> Again we ask that only those connected with the CW movement come to the retreat. . . . We are only anxious that you get the full benefit out of the conferences and that Brother Ass does not rebel before the week is out.

ON THE EVENING OF THE FIRST DAY OF THE RETREAT

> The sun is setting, orange and red between the cherry trees. The hills are misty blue. There is a real freshness in the air after another week of terrific heat. Sitting quietly in the little cabin before the first conference at 8.30. The crowd is gathering—representatives from many of the groups are here already.

TWO DAYS LATER (Notebook. N.d.)

So far everything has gone beautifully. Conferences on Confession, examination of conscience, contrition, Faith, Hope, and the Mass. All are keeping silence. . . . All our prayers are for peace."

ONE YEAR LATER

Dorothy again summons the community. A letter to fellow workers.

"O taste and see that the Lord is sweet." "With Thee is the fountain of life; from the stream of Thy delights Thou givest us drink. . . ." This is to remind you that the Pittsburgh retreats are July 4–10; 18–24; Aug 1–7; Aug 29 to Sept 4. They begin Sunday at 7.30, close Sat. at 3.00 p.m. For reservations write Retreat Master, St. Anthony's Village, Oakmont, Pa. The first three are for women but if you cannot get off for the last, write to Fr. [Louis] Farina at the above address. I am making the July 18th one. Today almost the whole staff went to 6 a.m. Mass and had breakfast together after. At 7.30 Jack Thornton and Mike Kovalak had to report at Grand Central for their army physical. Hazen [Ordway] left for the farm at Easton for the holiday. Tuesday he reports to the judge at Philadelphia for sentencing. Arthur and Smiddly left for the farm yesterday. It is very quiet around here today. Dave Mason is working on setting up Fr. Hugo's pamphlet, "The Weapons of the Spirit."

INSTRUCTIONS FOR PREPARING FOR A RETREAT
(A letter to fellow workers)

We can disturb the Holy Ghost by the senses, exterior and interior. There is no silence without silence of all senses. . . . Noises of the mind are the most dangerous of all. Shut out all plans, worries, memory. Forget the past. The will, the heart, must be focused on eternal life. Be calm about any decisions made during the week, about any spiritual problems. Convince yourself that the Holy Ghost is going to give you definite graces during the week. . . . Silence of the lips is the cheapest kind of silence. Silence is a gold mine. Then try to embrace all these other silences. As for graces, continually ask. Ask to be enlightened. Ask for light. . . . Keep asking.

THE IMPACT OF THE RETREAT

We were a little flock. We had broken bread together. Scripture became a love letter and retreat notes we took we kept rereading, going back to them to try to recapture that glow of rapturous assent to Truth.

Feeling our need, or was it to correct our distortions of doctrine, Fr. John J. Hugo began to write books on Nature and the Supernatural. . . . And of course the longing for love which is in every heart, entered in. Who has not experienced that "being in love" which suddenly intensified all joys, transformed one's surroundings, made all work interesting and full of meaning, made all things new, so that one saw the loved one as God sees him (and as we ought always to see all men.)

O, those first days of our conversion—and those first days of the retreat which was a second conversion for so many—how filled with the keenest happiness they were for us all. We were companions indeed, those of us who made the retreat.

FATHER HUGO COUNSELS AGAINST RIGORISM (Letter. N.d.)

First of all, it appears that a spirit of rigorism is creeping in among some of our friends in an excessive emphasis on external penance. . . . We should preach love rather than penance, penance simply as a means of progressing in love. And we should treat penance as secondary and supplementary. . . .

This rigorism shows itself in certain doctrinal exaggerations. For example: in the statement that all will be damned who do not *achieve* the degree of perfection to which they are predestined. Such a statement is erroneous and has no theological foundation. . . . I hope that you will be most careful in stating theological truths and will not betray yourself into any exaggerations by a temptation to startle or impress. The truth is startling enough.

Rigorism shows itself in a tendency to impose certain singularities of dress, of manner, of devotion. . . . It shows that they [retreatants] are confusing the shadow with the substance. Also, they are putting themselves in the proximate danger of spiritual pride, since they tend to regard all who do not adopt their singularities as imperfect or damned.

Finally, this rigorism is manifest in the desire to multiply habits of external devotion until souls lose all liberty and find their devotion a constraint and a burden. Let us not multiply devotions; let us teach people rather that every action is a devotion if done out of love for God. . . .

I do not know whether you have heard of, or been in contact with our rigorist friends, but this is to warn you since I cannot see you before the retreats.

FR. LACOUTURE TO DOROTHY (February 28, 1942. Retreat papers)

I am not surprised that you are causing a lot of concern to the officials, of both the state and the Church. It is a good sign. Was not Jesus condemned by his ecclesiastical superiors and civil authorities? Those who do His work must expect the same *reward*. P.S. If you come to Edmonton, it would be possible to see me, if you think it is worth such a long trip. But I advise you to wait till later on for at present I may not give any spiritual direction to anybody and that is the reason you would like to come, I suppose. I am bound to let you know that I am gagged by my superiors.

DOROTHY'S JUDGMENT OF FR. LACOUTURE

Dorothy did visit Father Lacouture and when he died on November 16, 1951, she attended his funeral. The following is the concluding paragraph of her editorial on Father Lacouture in the *Catholic Worker*, November 1961.

I should like to see on his gravestone the words "he made all things new," because his teaching of the love of God so aroused our love in turn, that a sense of the sacramentality of life was restored for us, and a new meaning and vigor was given to our lives.

2

Conversion

Dorothy's understanding of conversion was the traditional Catholic one. Conversion occurred when the person, out of gratitude for life and the hope of life fulfilled in eternity, turned to God and sought to do His will. The seeking went on as long as life—a continuous study, a continuous effort to enlighten understanding and then to will that understanding into the actions of one's life.

AN APPROXIMATE QUOTATION FROM ST. AUGUSTINE

This quotation appealed to Dorothy and she frequently used it.

> "Late Have I Loved Thee," and when I tell the story of my life and my conversion, it is a story of God's love for me and how it pursued me, not a story of my sins, my tortuous road thru life.

A REMEMBRANCE

Written at Tivoli, New York, September 24, 1967. This remembrance is an account of what to Dorothy were childhood signs of a predilection for conversion: an early disposition toward beauty, both of nature and of two fair faces.

It seems to me I have always had a sense of an immanent spiritual world. As a little child of eight, it was from reading the Bible, and going to a few Methodist services with a little friend next door to us in Oakland, California. The beauty of nature brought this to me. At the same time I remember passing a note to a little boy in school saying, "I love you," and the teacher keeping us both after school and probing us both to find the wickedness that my simple words were not meant to convey. I had merely thought he was beautiful. A year later when we had moved to Chicago after the earthquake of 1906 and I began to attend St. Mark's Church with the minister's daughter who was also named Dorothy, I remember the same admiration for a boy in the choir whose name was Russell. He sang beautifully and he looked like an angel.

THE BEACH EXPERIENCE. (Staten Island, 1925. Notes)

Dorothy used this statement on several different occasions.

I was "born again by the word of the Spirit," contemplating the beauty of the sea and the shore, wind and waves, the tides. The mighty and the minute, the storms and peace, wave and the wavelets of receding tides, sea gulls, and seaweed and shells, all gave testimony of a Creator, a Father almighty, made known to us through His Son. Jesus always seemed to have preferred following the seashore or the banks of some stream. . . . When in a strange land . . . [the apostles] had to procure their food somehow and . . . [they] undoubtedly supplied their wants from the produce of their fishing.

THE "INEXORABLE STATEMENT"

A statement relating to her own conversion which Dorothy often invoked.

"It is a terrible thing to fall into the hands of the living God."

CONVERSION AND COMMUNITY

My entire conviction at this time [of conversion] was that the Word is made Flesh today—the Incarnation is now. There is no true brotherhood of man unless we see Christ as our brother. The Word was in Scripture and in the Bread on the altar and I was to live by both. I *had* to live by both or wither away.

THE DESIRE FOR GOD

If we really desire God, by a miracle of grace He will lead us into the supernatural life where we have to live by faith. This is the desert, the place that is contrary to the world. Perhaps He will leave us without anything to eat and, like the Jews, we will call for meat. But we cannot argue about the love of God. Let us abandon self defense. Let us live the life of the desert of faith. Scouts will come back as they did to Moses and say it can't be done, but we must keep our mind on the Promised Land, on Heaven.

MASS CONVERSIONS

Father Denis Mooney being here reminds me I have been
thinking of St. Francis, St. Vincent Ferrer and mass conversions. This is what . . . [the women] at the Grail [a center
for training in the apostolate] think about. And Frank Duff
of the Legion of Mary. Lay workers all. Yet how impossible
it seems.

HOW THE JEWS [AND DOROTHY] SEE CONVERSION

In the Jewish view conversion is a development. We have to
be converted step by step.

3

Faith and the Senses

Dorothy, who sought "the hard contest" in her life of faith, strongly affirmed the position regarding "creatures" and the use of the senses on one hand, and faith on the other, that was a primary teaching of the retreat. The position was that "creatures," things, or objects, have value insofar as they testify to God's existence and enhance the glory of God. If they do not, if they become ends in themselves, they should be abandoned, for then they are only a part of vanity and corrupters of beauty. The same applies to the senses by which creatures are known. Their end is not objects, but God. They are the means to knowledge and the creation and apprehension of beauty. When the delectation of sense becomes the object of the person's impulse to knowledge and creativity, then these attributes of the human spirit lose their direction and become instruments of vanity and even, perhaps, of holocausts.

WHAT IS HUMAN DESTINY?

It is body and soul brought together with a marvelous unity. Beyond this God gives us further powers—a sharing in God's own nature, creativity. We are divinized. We can know, love God as He knows Himself, by faith here. Reason is perfected by faith. "We shall be like unto God, we shall see Him as He is." We shall be a new person, created

in grace. Therefore we must here begin to be made like to
Him.

FAITH

Faith is like walking from darkness into light and being
blinded by it.

THE STRUGGLE FOR FAITH

Faith does not make sense. In its initial forms it is easy to
get. This is enthusiasm at first. It is only when faith is tried
to the utmost that we truly give honor to God. Judge the
actions of life with the faith you have at the moment. God
is not going to reward us for the results of our faith but on
the love that is put into the effort. Faith is always seeing
further than reason but not contradicting it.

FAITH AND PREACHING

Faith is the action of the Holy Spirit on the souls of those
who listen to the word of God, Abbot Marmion said. Faith
comes from hearing, St. Paul said. Hearing and preaching.
Few of the apostles wrote. But we are all imperfect preach-
ers. We always give God's truth refracted.

FAITH AND UNDERSTANDING

The reward of faith is understanding. Therefore "seek not
to understand that thou mayest believe, but believe that
thou mayest understand." St. Augustine said this. I have

forgotten the name of the book [On *Free Choice,* II, 2, 6, is at least one source] which had this quotation, but it convinced me of the necessity of praying for those without faith rather than indulging in the futile attempt to make them understand.

SENSE AND THE LIFE OF THE SPIRIT

From sensual man we must grow into the spiritual in order to reach God. And the sensual man calls this foolishness, but one with faith calls it the folly of the Cross. We surrender the natural to gain the supernatural; we leave off sense gratification for spiritual light; the human for the divine; that which is of time for eternity; the earth for heaven; the world for God. When we disregard the rule that everything seeks to go higher, we are out of tune. We must accept the principle at the very beginning to surrender everything. We cannot compromise; we cannot water down the doctrine. Every attachment must be broken. If there are attachments, there is no possibility of advancement. We do not stand still. We go either forward or backward. The battleground of the spiritual life is in the small things.

JESUS AND THE SENSES

Knowing Jesus is difficult because life is so absorbing it becomes an obstacle. So we must sacrifice it. We must renounce so many of the things, the objects, the enticements, that are set before us today to show our preference for Jesus. We must give up our lives to save them. We must die to live. The devil urges us to use all of these things and enjoy them. The common language of the day is "there is no harm in it." But this is not true in most instances.

We are absorbed by the senses but Jesus is not of this

world. The life of Jesus contradicts ours. We must empty
our hearts of the things of sense so that we can develop the
vision of faith. Of course we approach our knowledge of
Christ thru the senses. But we must get past this as soon as
possible. The sooner the animal in us dies the angel in us
will find life.

FAITH AND SENSE

The senses look for an object, but joy is not where the
senses say it is. We must learn to abandon ourselves to
God.

MEDITATING ON THE LIFE OF OUR LORD

When we meditate on Our Lord's life we are meditating on
our own. God is to be found in what appears to be the little
and the unimportant. Don't look back 1900 years. Look
around us today. It is useless to try to make Christ's life
picturesque or interesting, humanly speaking. The great of
His time were not interested in Him. Our Lord took just
enough of the human to localize His Divinity. He wishes to
manifest Himself to the will, not to the emotions, or feelings. If His mysteries seem empty we must stay as Mary
Magdalene did at the empty tomb and He will reveal Himself.

WORLDLINESS

The great creative energy of our time is put to the end of
trying to perfect the means to lead a natural life. Principles
and forms of technology are being discovered which will
create a new level of existence for us. The ads are now filled

with the marvelous things we shall have after the war. So
we must try to train ourselves to build exactly our spiritual
edifice. Creatures have been thrown out of line. "Accursed
be the soil because of you." [Genesis 3:17]

DRUGS AND THE THINGS OF GOD

Our taste for creatures can become sated yet never satisfied.
The more we eat, the less we want, except in the instance of
drugs where the need seems always to increase. How curious, that as in drugs so it is in the things of God: our
capacity is always increasing. But do drugs lift the mind
and heart to God?

DOROTHY'S MORNING "SHOT IN THE ARM" (Notes. Undated. Ca. the late sixties)

I suppose you could call it [writing letters] a meditation
and it usually begins in my mind each day as I wake up
feeble with age and from noise and the duties of a large
family around me, here in the city and at the farm, scat-
tered over the country at home and abroad, and [this fam-
ily] communicating with me by mail. . . .

My strength, I must hasten to write, returns to me with a
cup of coffee and the reading of the psalms, sometimes one
or two, sometimes all of Matins and Lauds in the Divine
Office, complete, or in the short breviary, fortunately made
available to us all now. I do not question my motive, my
intention in this reading. Dr. Karl Stern [psychiatrist, author of *The Pillar of Fire* and a longtime friend of
Dorothy's] says there is too much self-analysis. The purist
would perhaps say that one should read the psalms in order
to pray, to offer praise and worship to God—not to revive
flagging spirits. But I need this shot in the arm, in order to

recognize that my first duty in life is to worship, to praise God for his creation, in order to get my mind straightened out so that I can see things in perspective.

A shot in the arm! Long years ago a communist friend of mine . . . made the comment when I said I did not have trouble going to sleep because as soon as I began to pray for everyone who crossed my thoughts, I fell asleep. "Religion is the opiate of the people," she said. And only a few years ago a drug addict who had the bed next to mine in the Woman's House of Detention where I was serving a fifteen day sentence for refusing to take shelter during an air raid drill, compulsory at the time in New York, made this remark: "when I wake up in the morning you are reading in that little book, and when I go to sleep at night you are reading it. Me, the first thing I think of in the morning and the last thing I think of at night is how when I get out I will get me a fix!"

"This is my fix," I told her, and I think she understood me. What she longed for was the beatific vision which we have glimpses of in this life, but which will only come after we pass that gateway which is death (a gateway through which we sometimes see the light streaming).

GOD ALONE

In the life of faith there is nothing for the senses. Only God alone. But our whole life seems to be to enjoy everything we can in this life. We stop at the material, the sensual, the physical life. They drown the soul. The carnal man cannot sense the things of the spirit. They are too far away. Faith is also needed.

THE DIVINE LIFE AND SPAGHETTI FOR LUNCH

Whether you eat or drink it is all for the glory of God. This does not mean we do not enjoy our spaghetti for lunch. God often gives us natural happiness to help us love Him. We do not give up spaghetti because we like it. We eat to nourish, to serve God because we love Him and we enjoy the food, its goodness, and thank Him for it.

THE FLESH

I want to write about our enemy the flesh, which is also our dear companion on this pilgrimage, our body, thru which we receive our greatest joys of body and spirit. Our senses convey to us knowledge of the truth; we hear of the truth, we hear of the faith with our ears, we see and understand things invisible thru things visible; we speak words of earthly love and eternal love (alas also words of ugliness and hate).

Our dear flesh, our good bodies which God made which begin to die even as we begin to live, ever dying, ever renewing, and finally decaying and being put into the ground like grains of wheat to rise again with new life at the last day. "I believe in the resurrection of the body and life everlasting."

Brother Ass, St. Francis called our body, and what burdens it must bear of joy and sorrow, what torrents of pleasure pass over it; into what an abyss of pain it can fall.

A woman contemplates her body, "that earthen vessel," that temple of the Holy Ghost, and young or old, it is always holy. Young, it is as fresh and fragrant as flowers. Old, it is worn and stale; there is the smell of age and corruption about it. But this aging flesh, I love it. I treat it tenderly, but also I rejoice that it has been well used. Had my vocation been that of a wife and mother I would have given myself to my husband and children, and then my flesh, well used, would droop and my breasts sag but my eyes and lips would rejoice and love and laugh with happiness.

Or, if I had remained a single woman, a virgin, would I have willingly cast myself into the arms of God or have longed for earthly love, and then have it pass me by?

But God has chosen me and "blessed are those who have not seen but believed" in this love, this terrible overwhelming cruelly demanding love of the living God.

THE HOLINESS OF THE FLESH

Our Lord performed cures through contact with his sacred humanity. . . . It is characteristic of the Son of Man to will that cure should come from contact with his sacred flesh. During his life it was the exception when he healed at a distance. "He, laying his hands on them, healed them." There was not a word about whether or not they deserved to be healed. They came to him. That was enough. He healed them.

THE DUTY OF CHRISTIANS

Today imposes with a particular stress on everyone the duty to flee other blandishments of the world, to renounce unrestrained pleasures of the body, any formality or vanity which does not get us to heaven.

EXISTENCE: THE PSYCHOLOGICAL PLANE VERSUS THE SPIRITUAL PLANE

The following was handwritten on December 19, 1959, in Dorothy's "Notebook." It makes the point that a psychological adaptation of the person to the necessities of time and sense dims, if not obliterates, a spiritual vision. While the thought is certainly of her own mind, the writing style is not. But nowhere in this text are there quotation marks. Dorothy does indicate her source, however, as René Voillaume, Abbot-general of The Little Brothers of Jesus before and during the period of World War II. According to Sister Peter Claver, Voillaume was, among the modern writers on the spiritual life, the one on whom Dorothy placed her greatest emphasis. Toward the end of her life Dorothy gave to Sister her copy of Voillaume's works—filled, Sister says, with Dorothy's marginal notes.

> Sensual . . . love blinds the spirit which is striving to love God. Our vocation more than any other places us at the heart of the contradiction of the world in the very place where it is most violent because we are placed at the point where the contemplation of the invisible and crucified God is forced to implant itself in the daily activities of men. We will not find any unity of life around us and we will not come to question the principle of it in ourselves unless we free ourselves from dependence on the world, from our sensitive nature, raising ourselves above the psychological plane.
>
> Those who wish to realize unity on a psychological plane of their life cannot attempt it without the risk of destroying the supernatural élan of their deepest life.

THE COMMUNITY OF GOD

One of the great problems today is that we have ourselves taken over the process of creating. So when we begin to create or not create according to our own self-interest it is like the sorcerer's apprentice. We do not know when to stop and fantastic things occur. So we should remember that all things that are made are made for Him. In Him we live and have our being and all creating should be for God and His glory.

God wishes to glorify Himself in me. We must carry this glory in our lives so that when our neighbors touch us, they have contact with God. In giving I have more. "That they all may be one, the glory thou has given me, I have given them." This was the last prayer of Christ. We are all apostles too. We must be perfected in unity, that the world may know Thou has loved them.

4

Death and Immortality

The belief in a personal immortality was the inviolable center of that equation which, for the individual, began in time and ended in eternity. Any completed logic which applied to existence absolutely required this belief. To say that "all" was an accident was an assault on the person so profound that the phrase itself could have no meaning whatever. If there was no immortality, then, as Dostoyevsky's Ivan had said, "all is permitted." In Dorothy's notes was another quotation on immortality from Dostoyevsky which she apparently believed to be true since she herself often restated the idea in the quotation in the form of a question. How could one love "mankind," the "masses," without first affirming the unique and eternal character of every created person? Dostoyevsky's statement is quoted in Henri De Lubac's *The Drama of Atheistic Humanism.*

> I declare that love for mankind is something completely inconceivable, incomprehensible, and even impossible without faith in the immortality of the human soul.

DEATH

> Instead of fearing death, which changes nothing, we should fear life. This is because those who wish to enter heaven must be saints. Sanctity must be achieved in our lifetime.

We are here for no other reason. We are not changed in Purgatory. We are cleansed. . . . If we wish the joy of Heaven, we must cultivate a taste for it here.

MEDITATION IN A CEMETERY (Rossville, Long Island, August 9, 1953. Notes)

We have been visiting the cemetery several times a week. . . . I never thought it would be a happy occasion—visiting cemeteries, but the little cemetery on a gentle hill back of St. Joseph's Church . . . is a happy spot.

Little Charlie Smith's grave is in the far left-hand corner, in the southeast corner. There is a park bench beside the Catholic Worker plot, and when we have arranged our vases of flowers, we sit on the bench and eat the pears we have gathered from the next field and say the rosary. There is Mrs. Smith, and Bernadette, and Lucille, and Mac, and the neighbor's children, Janet and Artie, and my grandchildren, Becky, Susie, Eric, Nick and Mary. Back of us is the . . . St. Joseph's [plot and] down the way fifty feet is the Marist Fathers' and there Brother Philip, a friend of Tamar's and mine, is buried. He was the hero of the story "The Brother and the Rooster," which I wrote for the *Commonweal* years ago, and which is included in their collection—The Commonweal Reader. . . .

It is quiet but for the sound of crickets, katydids and an occasional cicada, and the August sun covers everything with a dusty gold.

I used not to be able to understand Clotilde's predilection for the cemetery in Léon Bloy's *The Woman Who Was Poor,* but now I do. Life and death are so close together. Little Charlie Smith was drowned July 11. Baby Margaret was born exactly 4 weeks later. "The spaces of our life, set over against eternity, are brief and poor."

PURGATORY

Once Christ is in my soul then Heaven begins. The germ of glory should normally develop so that the flame of charity would burn out all of the stain of sin. We should not have to go to purgatory if we thought straight. One cannot merit there. We do violence to our very nature to think of going there. To see God face-to-face immediately after death is the right way to look at things. According to the fundamental law of grace, the sufferings I go thru now are meritorious, so we should generously suffer purgatory here where there is a chance to merit.

THE REACH FOR IMMORTALITY—THE INADEQUACY OF REASON

I believed in order that I might understand, St. Anselm said. "It is reasonable to believe," I frequently hear. I will of course use my reason as far as it will take me, and must enlighten it as one must one's conscience, but there comes a time, very often, when one must live on blind and naked faith. "I believe. Help thou, O God, my unbelief." In this dark night, or in this desert, I know as others have known, that God sends intimations of immortality. We receive enough light to keep going, to follow the path. And I believe that if the will is right, God will take us by the hair of the head, as he did Habbakuk, who brought food to Daniel in the lion's den, and will restore us to the Way and no matter what our wandering, we can still say, "All is Grace."

THE RESURRECTION OF THE BODY

This reflection from "The Apology of Saint Justin Martyr" [A.D. 150] was copied by Dorothy, no doubt for reading and rereading.

> If you were not such as you are, nor of such an origin, and anyone should show you the generating substance, and a painted representation of the human form, and should persist in affirming that the one could be produced from the other, would you believe him before you saw the effect produced? No one would be bold enough to assert that he would. In the same manner you now disbelieve because you never saw a dead man raised to life. But even, as you would not at first have believed that from a little drop of seminal matter such bodies could be formed, which yet you see are formed, so consider that it is not impossible for human bodies, decomposed and like seed dissolved into the earth to arise in due season at the command of God and to put on incorruption.

DEATH (From "Notebook," December 19, 1959)

> Visits during the month—one from the father and son of the little family which lost the young mother with cancer. They came to me before her death, all of them, and told me. And the little girl looked at me and said, "My mother is going to heaven."
>
> What courage! What faith and hope! To be facing the great moment in our lives which is sure to come. We are all under sentence of death. And it may be "sooner than we think." . . . How much does death and the life which follows appear as something which makes a man grow. This is the mystery of our life. The thought of death should be our strength and greatness. Only man of all the creatures

knows that he must die. The preparation for death is an essential part of [my] monthly day of recollection.

THE RESURRECTION

Our Lord appealed to His resurrection to attest His divinity. Just after he commissions Peter to his Church, Matthew says (16:21): "From that time Jesus began to make it clear to his disciples that he was destined to go to Jerusalem and suffer grievously at the hands of the elders and chief priests and scribes, to be put to death and to be raised up on the third day." In John (10:18) Christ says: "The Father loves me, because I lay down my life in order to take it up again. No one takes it from me; I lay it down of my own free will, and as it is in my power to lay it down, so it is in my power to take it up again." Then Paul says (Philippians 3:20): "For us, our homeland is in heaven, and from heaven comes the savior we are waiting for, the Lord Jesus Christ, and he will transfigure these wretched bodies of ours into copies of his glorious body. He will do that by the same power with which he can subdue the whole universe."

These are pledges for our hope. We are one body with Christ, as St. Paul says. We all sinned in Adam and in ourselves, yet we will be restored. Here, our soul is subject to the body. In Heaven the body will be subject to the soul, not to the limitations of time and space.

We should not, then, try to glorify our body here.

THE HOPE FOR HEAVEN

By fixing our mind on our eternal destiny we . . . put our heart in Heaven. Then we begin *now* to experience Heaven. We enjoy in anticipation—that is *hope*. Hope is a foretaste of Heaven. St. Francis lived in such anticipation of Heaven that he left creatures where they were and only took them when he needed them—never to satisfy his senses. He was happy because he was in love.

THE WILLINGNESS TO DIE FOR GOD

This quotation from St. Ignatius of Antioch was copied by Dorothy and found in her miscellaneous papers.

> I am writing to all the churches to tell them all that I am, with all my heart, to die for God—if only you do not prevent it. I beseech you not to indulge your benevolence at the wrong time. Please let me be thrown to the wild beasts. Through them I can reach God. I am God's wheat; I am the pure bread of Christ, ground by the teeth of the wild beasts. . . .
>
> And even when I am come, if I should beseech you, pay no attention to what I say; believe, rather, what I am writing to you now. . . . Farewell and persevere to the end in Jesus Christ.

HEAVEN (Notes. N.d.)

Heaven is when we see God face to face, when we shall see Him as He is. Now it is only a glimpse, a suggestion of light, of joy, of unity, of completion.

5

The Church and the Cross

Occasionally Dorothy would refer to herself as "a daughter of the Church." By this she meant a union of her mind and spirit with the Church that went far beyond the state of simply being "comfortable" in it. To her, the Church was a reality that had pierced history, channeling its glory into time's dark and aimless wanderings by its sacramental life and by its teaching that existence could be freed from time's slavery and returned to light. It was the source of life—all life—and it, as she said, provided her with "an instruction and way of life" to which, for all of her years, she gave an undeviating fidelity.

THE EUCHARIST

Many times this has occurred to me. What a preposterous statement Jesus made when he said, "Take, eat, this is my body. Take, drink, this is my blood. Unless you eat the body and drink the blood of the son of man ye shall not have life in you."

And many went away scandalized. They could not take it. We can only take it if we do not think about it. Only if it becomes a routine can we bear it from day to day. . . .

I believe that the humanity of Christ is present in the morsel of bread kept in the tabernacles of our churches (as

the Jews kept the manna sent by God) and I believe because these are the words of Christ himself.

GOING TO COMMUNION

Why is it so many can go to daily communion and yet there
is so little change in us? Our communion is to give us
strength and grace for the day, and we lose it by our selfishness. Instead of grace increasing in us, it is received in vain.
This is a scandal to others.

LOVE OF THE CHURCH

As for me I love the Church who has room for saints and
sinners, for the mediocre, the lame, the halt and the blind.
The great diversity in the Church gave me a feeling that I
was truly welcome in it and I still like the expression Holy
Mother Church. Even as I write this I think of that big
warm motherly soul in Steinbeck's *Grapes of Wrath,* who
sits by the side of her son who is driving the broken down
truck from one field of work to another, defeated for the
moment by the miseries of their lot, but not conquered,
fulfilling her woman's role of keeping the family of man
together, in a life which can indeed be considered a vale of
tears, but a life, too, filled with the most intense joys which
go hand in hand with sorrow and suffering, in both the
natural and supernatural order. . . .

"Sick of the Church, sick of religion." The desert Fathers
themselves complained of it and called it acedia, defined in
the dictionary as spiritual sloth and indifference. And the
remedy for that, according to spiritual writers, is faithfulness to the means to overcome it, recitation of the psalms
each day, prayer and solitude, and by these means arriving,
or hoping to arrive, at a state of well being. . . .

To pray the psalms . . . even without understanding. . . . Then suddenly like a sudden shower, understanding of a verse comes, with the light of joy like sun breaking through the clouds.

THE GLORY OF THE MASS (The *Catholic Worker*, March 1966)

To me the Mass, high or low, is glorious and I feel that though we know we are but dust, at the same time we know too, and most surely through the Mass, that we are little less than the angels, that indeed it is not I but Christ in me worshipping, and in Him I can do all things, though without Him I am nothing. I would not dare write or speak or try to follow the vocation God has given me to work for the poor and for peace if I did not have this constant reassurance of the Mass.

ATTENDING MASS

One cannot be said to go to Mass to satisfy one's aesthetic sense. Or for the kicks. It is a duty and an obligation to come together in community to praise, honor, worship, thank the good Lord and to beg the strength to continue the daily round, bear the daily sufferings of our human condition.

THE BLESSED SACRAMENT (Notes. N.d.)

How often I feel that a solid tide of evil is held off from us by the Blessed Sacrament in our midst, here at the farm, and by our daily Communion at St. Joseph. We hold it back, it is dissolved like a mist by the Sun of Justice.

GOING TO MASS

The Mass is the most important thing we do.

TRANSUBSTANTIATION

Down in the chicken house [at the Easton farm, WW II] the incubator chicks are hatching out. Mr. Lang showed me the sharp steel-like points on their beaks which grew there just to release them from the shell and afterwards fall off. Day-old chicks can go without food and water because the yolk forms their stomachs and its absorption suffices them for food, Mr. Lang says.

Such miracles we see all around us, which we accept too readily. Yet no-one can explain or produce life. Yet so many will not accept transubstantiation!

BAPTISM, A DIRECTION TOWARD THE DIVINE LIFE

At baptism divine life is grafted onto human. Divine life is a gift. How do we reconcile all these elements of life? In the person these lives do not exist separately. That which in us is of the divine must dominate the rest, but due to the condition of human nature it is almost inevitable that natural impulses, the Adam life, should take over. All of these impulses, eating, sleeping, walking, talking, knowing, thinking, loving—all should be brought into harmony and regulated by human reason. But there is a higher rule than reason. By baptism we were given higher powers. Not reason alone, but faith ruling reason, governs our life.

These human activities by their nature tend to get us somewhere. They have their reward. They have their destination. As Newman said, "What a tragedy not to have begun to live." Our Adam life will not get us to Heaven. Baptism compels us to further Divine life in us. But it does not follow that because I possess divine life I automatically live it and it will get me into Heaven. It gives me freedom to use my will. I must desire Heaven. Every day of our lives we must further the Christ life in us. "For I know that in my flesh no good dwells. . . . For the inclination of the flesh is death."

How to go about the business of loving God? Our actions are expressions of the love that is in us. It is out of our common lives, filled with ordinary actions, that we are supposed to increase in love, to become saints. By using the graces in our souls, in doing dishes, floors, raising children —these must be done for the love of God. We must withdraw our love gradually from all else and do all for the love of God. It is not enough just to avoid mortal sin. One does not marry to avoid adultery. Abraham would never have been able to do things God's way unless he had had much practice all of his life. That is why so much emphasis must be placed on little things.

We love the world's goods—body goods and soul goods —outside of God. But Christ said blessed are your poor. Woe to you rich. Blessed are those who accept their poverty. Christ is always in opposition to the Adam world. Blessed are the meek, those who know how to suffer well. Love your enemies who rob you of earthly happiness of the sort that can keep you from heavenly happiness.

THE BAPTISM OF DESIRE

Love is the baptism of desire. Anyone who loves God belongs to the soul of the Church.

BAPTISM AND DEATH

Baptism does not automatically produce happiness. It does not rob us of our freedom. The love of God grows only in life. Death will not change anything in our lives. When we die we do not stop loving the world and then become passionate lovers of God. The more we cultivate a taste for God now, the more we have at the moment of death. The only thing that survives is love, and baptism consecrates us to that end.

THE CROSS

The Cross is the instrument of Christ's suffering and death. It stands at the center of time, a stark and forbidding sign of the evil that time can spawn. It is the point of deposit for all of the suffering and all of the death that was or will be. But God, by Himself suffering and dying on the Cross, transformed its dark and torturous meaning into light.

The Cross is the portal into beauty, into eternity. There is no figure of human conception so exalted as the Cross, for from out of its desolation life receives its highest due.

EVIL

Is God responsible for evil? God, who is all good, cannot be the cause of evil. But He allows it and being God He draws good out of it. "All things work together unto those who love God." Nothing escapes Him. He sustains in existence those who are doing evil. Evil is the deprivation of good. The devil himself works on human beings. God permits it

RING

the joy of heaven. Christ suffered to redeem us and to set us
an example for our own suffering. We therefore should not
be embittered when we suffer, whether from sickness or
from people injuring us. The lives of the saints are filled
with their suffering. Our enemies are the galley slaves that
row us unto heaven. We should love our enemies as we are
enjoined to do because they make us unto saints. . . .

By nature we tend to increase in selfishness but suffering
can do away with it. There is no sanctity separated from
suffering. God will give me the grace to bear it.

SUFFERING AND PRAYER (Notebook. February 24, 1972)

How suffering drives us to prayer. I mean mental suffering
caused by . . . those you love. But it seems that to love is
to suffer. One must constantly recall the necessity to grow
in confidence in God. The word [confidence] means with
faith, so suffering is an opportunity to grow in faith. Confidence, trust, trust in one another too. Trust that prayers
will be answered. . . . To love is to suffer. Perhaps our
only assurance that we do love God, Jesus, is to accept this
suffering.

SUFFERING AND THE "HARD CONTEST"

Paul was knocked to earth off his horse. If we receive the grace of humility we become blind, we must proceed by faith. Our Lord spent thirty years hidden—forty days in the desert. We hear much of the activities of saints but little of their solitude and affliction of body and soul. The trouble is we do not want mystical graces. We want Our Lord to come into our souls without suffering. If we murmur or complain we are frustrating God's work. We may be fed milk in the early days, but God wants to give us the meat of the strong. So if God leaves us in darkness, in illness, or seems to be a contradiction, God must be very near. [Then, quoting a Bishop Bossuet, Dorothy asks, what can be gained] "from our worldly Christians and their fashionable piety. If suffering be necessary, give us back a Nero."

SUFFERING AND THE MOTHER OF GOD

Mary was a witness and participant in the crucifixion of Christ. She is the mother of all those who suffer. Mary stands between us and divine justice. She will help us to bear it, to discover that the Cross is sweet. She is the mother of the Mystical Body and a mother bears the pain of those whom she has begotten. We must grow through Mary. She will be with us in Bethlehem and at our Calvary. She is the way to put on Christ. She begot us on Calvary.

CHRIST'S SUFFERING AND SENSE OF ABANDONMENT

On Calvary Christ cried out "My God, My God" out of the desolation that came from a sense of separation from

God. This was His greatest struggle and in our own lives it gives us an insight into the frightful consequences of sin. Still, if we suffer from a sense of abandonment, cry out to God. Tell Him that we are willing to suffer. Then tell Him all our problems like children to their mother. But . . . only as we advance in our love of God do we feel the sense of abandonment. So it is permissible to ask relief, to promise to praise Him. *Thy will be done.* He wants us to be lifted up on the Cross of detachment.

On the Cross Heaven was shut to Him, yet he still prays and invokes the glory of His Father.

WHY SUFFERING?

It was not in the plan of God that we should suffer. He placed the first man and woman in Paradise. Suffering was the permanent injury that was the result of original sin. Original sin was, in a sense, the corollary of freedom—the freedom of the will. With freedom, there had to be suffering. . . . Suffering gives us an understanding of the malice of sin.

Most of us have not really suffered. Suffering seems cruel, unjust. It is a scandal to us. But God can make us understand by meditating upon and knowing His own passion. Love reveals itself to love. To enter into His suffering is to enter into His love.

From the standpoint of our reason the Passion is weakness, folly, humiliation. Christ was completely subject to His enemies—this is all we see with our mind, the wounds and bruises of one who came to cure and heal. He came to give life and he dies. He came as the King of Kings and was treated as nothing. One word from Him would have stopped this, yet He did not open his mouth.

From reason we cannot understand this. For four thousand years God had been preparing for His coming. Empires had been overthrown, prophets sent, and His own power demonstrated. Christ showed His power when He said, "The Father loves me, because I lay down my life in order to take it up again. No one takes it from me; I lay it down of my own free will and as it is in my power to lay it down, so it is in my power to take it up again."

When God sends us suffering it is to give us wisdom. Think of His power and you will be able to endure His weakness. When you meditate in weakness, the mountain of your own pride will be leveled, the sun of your natural inclinations will be darkened.

Our Lord showed us what it cost to get back Heaven lost for a trifle, like Esau. Our Lord teaches us the value of Heaven by the price He paid for it. Through the example of His passion we will learn to obtain it.

Treasure the memory of His passion because it is His wish. Our sacraments flow from the fountain of the Cross. It was the means of saving the world, the symbol and doctrine of our faith.

THE PARADOX OF THE CROSS

Salvation is in the Cross. It was the instrument of Christ's degradation; it is also the instrument of our salvation. The Cross means the crucifixion of the Adam life. The Cross is the law of our life. If we wish to live, we must die. As Newman said, "We must defraud [human] nature at times in order not to be defrauded of grace." Christianity is not a religion of mortification but is one of the love of Christ. Yet both go together. In order to love Christ, one must deny oneself.

HUMILITY

Humility means self-annihilation. My God and my all—all for the glory of God . . . that God may be glorified in all things. This disposition must become ingrained into us—a habit of mind—a subconscious presence like a person in love.

There are guides to this "habit" of humility. There should be a pure intention. We must have humility before ourselves. We should never compare ourselves to others. Only to God. The Sacred Heart is a symbol of Christ's self-annihilation. A devotion to the Sacred Heart means self-annihilation. We must lose the art of self-defense. We must be washed from attachments. Attachments come on the soul like dust on windows.

MERCY

This is the one mark of the Christian to which Christ gives the most expression. The quality of mercy depends on its motive. It can be dictated by policy, duty, politics, pity, or natural softness of the heart. But genuine mercy should come from the motive of love, which seeks the good of another and grieves over suffering as if one suffers himself. In Ecclesiastes it says that "He will not break the bruised reed, nor quench the smoking wick." We have assurance that there is no wickedness too great for His mercy. Sin gives us a title to his mercy. The misuse of free will is the only barrier.

AUTHORITY

In the Church, one certainly would not seek after authority. But if, through ability, it is thrust upon one, as it was on St. Peter, St. Ambrose, Pius XII and countless others, . . . then it would seem necessary to cultivate humility, courage, holy indifference, holy poverty, in order to fulfill one's high office. To have authority is to lead by example. Even St. Francis, humblest, poorest of saints, was thrust into a position of authority.

GRACE

The grace tie goes on into eternity. The blood tie ends with death.

6

Love

It is remarkable that Dorothy, in whose natural disposition were strong elements of self-assertiveness, contentiousness, and even combativeness, should be recognized as one of the eloquent voices of this era to speak for love as the ultimate reality in which all of the world's turbulence, pain, and hate could forever be resolved.

THE CONSOLATION OF GOD'S LOVE

St. John of the Cross talks of the involuntary pleasure which comes about when the soul is caressed by God and how it overflows into the senses. Is this an experience of that love? All my prayer, my own sufferings, my reading, my study, would lead me to this conclusion.

Love is a great and holy force and must be used as a spiritual weapon. Put love against hate, suffering against violence. What is two thousand years in the history of the world? We have scarcely begun to know Christ, to see Him in others around us. With what kind of love did Mary Magdalene love our lord; how intense was the love of the Blessed Mother; how all-encompassing the love of St. John who rested his head on the breast of Jesus? All love is holy —the love of passion, of friendship—there is passion in it all, for passion means suffering. In David's life there was

the love of Jonathan. He loved him passing the love of
woman. They were one soul. Every kind of love is portrayed in the life of David, with all the attendant temptations of our disordered flesh. The love of friends, of father,
of husband, of the old man, and finally for the young
Shunammite who lovingly tended him in his old age. He
was a type of Christ, he was a forerunner, and his was a
very human life so that he even fell into great sin. . . . All
these things are written for our instruction and yet when
we experience the depths of love, when our love is leading
us on, we are afraid, and tremble, and human respect too
enters in.

Love is so beautiful and lust so ugly. And all the world is
busy portraying lust—that of the two small boys in *The
Lost Weekend,* that of the millhands in *God's Little Acre,*
that of the aging evangelist in *Tobacco Road*—it is in us all.
Self-deceit may make us try to cover it up but just as the
corruption of the flesh is there, the rottenness of decay, the
seed of death—so also is the seed of everlasting life.

So I will not be afraid, and I will talk of love and write of
love, and God help me, I will suffer for it too—the humilia-
tions, the degradations, the misunderstandings—because
"what is it I love when I love my God?"

So one does not mind being considered a fool. There is
the story of Prince Myshkin's love for Aglaia and Na-
stasya, not a love of passion but of compassion. There are
Sara, Rachel, Rebecca—they were old and they were loved.
Love comes at any age, and the remembrance, the nostalgia
is there. And yet who would go back to the agonies of
youth? No, it is a happy thing, a joyous thing to think of
the love to come, the love of God which awaits us, the
fulfillment where we will know as we are known, when all
our talents, energies, abilities will be utilized and developed, when we will be truly loved.

A SPRINGTIME THOUGHT ON LOVE

Spring, sap rising, weather raw but something in the air—growth. Fall mild and beautiful, spring restless. Love, the desire for love—we are made for love, at fifty, at eighty—a child's love, an embrace, a man's head on one's breast. [It all will be fulfilled in the] Resurrection of the body. Remember [this] last end [when] thy youth shall be restored as the eagle's.

LOVE OF BROTHER

St. John never disassociated the love of Christ and the love of brother. "As I have loved you," we are to love one another. This is the great commandment. *I love God as much as I love the one I love least.*

DETRACTION

They made their charges against Jesus and He was silent: a blasphemer, one having a devil, breaker of the Sabbath, [one who] went with publicans and sinners.

There is no lie like a half lie; no calumny more cruel than truth which hides falsehood. St. Ignatius says a thing must always be taken as meant by the author. . . . Never pass on things you hear. Lie it die with you. Evil tongues do threefold evil. They do harm to the one who speaks, the one who listens, and the one about whom it is said. Accept all of this for oneself beforehand. Know that this is coming. "If you need an advocate, God will send you one." Our Lady said nothing to St. Joseph. God had to settle the problem. We are what we are in the sight of God. . . . If we want peace, we must use these means. This is the only victory. We must work in our own small way. Daily communicants should stop all back-biting, slander, gossip, and make peace where we [they] are.

DEVELOPING LOVE IN OURSELVES

The way we generate love in ourselves and in others, too, is by having to exercise faith. We are deepening our own love and we make it possible for us to influence others in real love. . . . Disgust, failure, discouragement, ingratitude, all make us exercise our faith. Monotony, too. These four form a large part of our relationship with others. We have the opposite emotions, but these are most important because they generate Divine Love. They are, actually, fruitful and golden opportunities, for real happiness comes when we can be faced with a situation that ordinarily brings these reactions, and still remain interiorly peaceful. That is what grace is given for, so we must use it. Then we shall come to an overflow of pleasantness, success, encouragement, but on the Divine level. A Christian is never disgusted, or feels failure, or becomes discouraged. A true Christian does not feel that anyone owes him any gratitude; nothing is ever monotonous when we are always doing what God wishes. Love is never a monotonous but an eternal thing.

Humanly speaking, we turn away from things like disgust, failure, discouragement, and ingratitude, and turn toward pleasure. There is nothing in our human nature that will draw us towards these things. It has to be done by grace, which is a gratuitous gift of Almighty God. First we have to appreciate it, then beg for grace. . . .

The greatest favor you can do any person is to accept all these things from him. Then, of course, you are doing at the same time the greatest possible favor to yourself. You can never say you love a person until you have tasted all these things from him, and still we love him for the joy that we get from him.

This doctrine is hard. It is the pathway of the cross, and learning it is a life-time job.

PRIDE

Pride comes as soon as we begin to compare ourselves with others, for on this vertical plane we can always manage to feel superior. But God is all. We are nothing.

BEING "IN LOVE"

When will I learn to love all, men and women, with an intense awareness of their beauty, their virtues, strengths—to see them as Christ sees them?

Being "in love" is a sample of what love can mean in its discernment, in its "knowing" the other. It is a sample of the love of God. It is intense of body and soul, yet pure. "For thee my soul thirsteth, for thee my flesh longeth, O now exceedingly." We are without sex, all of us when we say at each meal, "Behold the handmaid of the Lord, be it done unto me according to thy word."

A FEELING OF BEING LOVED (Notes. June 16, 1966)

I awoke this morning with the feeling, very strong—I belong to someone to whom I owe devotion. I recalled an early love and that joyous sense of being not my own, but of belonging to someone who loved me completely.

THE WORD "LOVE"

It is a word which attracts, of which one is never tired. It cannot, in its right meaning, be cheapened, degraded, or coarsened. All want it, like David and Jonathan, Ruth, Esther—people.

LOVE IN ACTION

To put love into action, we must do all for the love of God. It is out of our common lives, filled with ordinary actions, that we are supposed to increase in love, to become saints.

LEVELS OF LOVE

This reflection, written in a small spiral-bound notebook, appears to have been composed while traveling—perhaps in a bus station.

I should be afraid to write about love because I have seen the terrible things it can do to you, but I have set out upon the path and I cannot turn back now. Especially now when I begin to learn what it means, the length and depth of it, the terror, the deep peace, the joy. No, there is nothing else worth writing about. What are all our lives about, what are we looking for, what do we want of each other? There is not one of us who has not gone thru the first stages of love and found them so enchanting that never in all our lives can we go further. Always we want to stand in that first light, that first fullness of life and let it possess us utterly. And when love would take us on thru the darkness which is light unutterable, we are blind and can go no further. We hold back. We clutch at our memory, and our own understanding of love and refuse to be taught.

But we had better look out! There are two dangers. We either fall into a snare of pleasure—sink into the immanence of love, or we presume, we fly too high—and in our confusion get lost in the transcendence of love.

We presume. We pray for love. We get it and it comes in strange forms and ways and we are likely to pass it by in pride or find ourselves grasping phantoms. . . .

If only we did not struggle. It only we did not make a move. We throw our own perverse wills into the balance and there are strange results in this search for love. You see it everywhere, on Broadway and 42nd St.—love, sex, pleasure, tenderness, fellowship, light, warmth, gaiety. It is all so bound up together even on this low level. Or you might go still lower and find it in the teenage gangs, the neighborhood clubs, the brothels, the lust for money to get women, to get love.

It is sad—it is horrible—but it is not to be despised. Should we hate and judge our brothers, we who also want to love?

Even in the perversity, so openly spoken of today, there too is the search for love. When we search for love in creatures, when we turn from God to creatures, instead of seeking God *in* creatures, then all is perversity. There is no natural love, or unnatural love, nor human sin, or inhuman sin, as people try to flatter themselves. "I'm just human!" "I'm not a pervert."

Oh, if God would only compel us to live quietly, to know that underneath are the everlasting arms.

7

Sanctity

Once the process of conversion had begun, there was no end to that process except sanctity. The struggle for sanctity was a work which, from surface appearance, few people could have found more onerous than Dorothy did. Yet perhaps few people have taken up that work with more steadfast determination than she, driven as she was by the conviction that the objective was worth whatever sacrifice and struggle had to be made to achieve it. Sanctity was the true work of her life, the "hard contest" that she had wanted.

ONE ROUTE TO HELL

If we imitate the imperfections of the saints we are liable to go to hell.

CALLED TO BE SAINTS (A pamphlet reprint from an editorial in the *Catholic Worker*)

We are either on the road to heaven or hell. "All the way to heaven is heaven, for He said I am the Way," St. Catherine of Siena tells us. And likewise all the way to hell is hell. . . .

It is the retreat as given at Maryfarm—the call to perfection of all Christians. It is again this idea that has been stressed in the columns of the *Catholic Worker*—we are called to be saints.

It is so tremendous an idea that it is hard for people to see its implications. Our whole literature, our culture, is built on ethics, the choice between good and evil. The drama of the ages is on this theme. We are still living in the Old Testament, with commandments as to the natural law. We have not begun to live as good Jews, let alone as good Christians. . . . We are cannibals.

In all secular literature it has been so difficult to portray the good man, the saint, that a Don Quixote [Cervantes, *Don Quixote]* is a fool; that Prince Myshkin [Dostoyevsky, *The Idiot]* is an epileptic in order to arouse the sympathy of the reader, appalled by unrelieved sanctity. . . .

Too little has been stressed the idea that *all* are called. Too little attention has been placed on the idea of mass conversions. . . . There have been in these days mass conversions to nazism, fascism, and communism.

DO PROTESTANTS HAVE ANY SAINTS? (Notes. February 22, 1959)

Went to Mass at eight, driven by a young man who was going with an intelligent young Lutheran girl and he kept telling me how he argued with her. Did the Protestants have any saints?—No. Did the Blessed Mother visit any of them?—No. Etc. I felt like saying that Catholics needed them more.

SANCTITY AND ORDINARY PEOPLE

All are called to be saints. Not to do the extraordinary—if sanctity depended on doing the extraordinary, there would be few saints.

THE NEED FOR SAINTS NOW

There is room for greater saints now than ever before. Never has the world been so organized, press, radio, education, recreation, to turn minds away from Christ. St. Paul was converted when he had murder in his mind. We are all called to be saints. God expects something from each one of us that no one else can do. If we don't, it will not be done.

THE SAINTS AND THE LIFE TODAY

We are not quite sure where we are going. The saints all knew the plan of God. Christians now do not accept self-denial. We are ready enough to see the evils of the world around us. We can name them all, but not the remedy. We make a diagnosis like a doctor who goes thru a ward and does nothing but ask for his fee. If we live Christ's way we have a remedy. We must plan to build our skyscraper from earth to heaven.

It was, apparently, during the summer of 1943 that Dorothy decided that she should make a more determined effort in her work for progress in the life of the spirit. This decision resulted in her solitary retreat at the Dominican Sisters' orphanage at Farmingdale, Long Island. Extracts from her notebook for this period tell of her decision to go and of the consequences of this experience.

THE DECISION TO LEAVE THE ACTIVE LIFE

The world is too much with me in the Catholic Worker. The world is suffering and dying. I am not suffering and dying in the Catholic Worker. I am writing and talking about it.

Of course I will not save my soul alone. Wherever we are we are with people. We drag them down or pull them up. Or we get dragged down or pulled up. And in recognition of this latter fact, I recognize also the need for aids and counsels in the path to God.

That is why as soon as possible I will try to organize days of recollection—primarily for myself. I will not be able to stand the impact of the world otherwise. But that will mean others—how many, who can tell? And later, retreats. We can do nothing today without saints, big ones and little ones. The only weapons we will develop will be those of prayer and penance. And the world will leave us alone, saying, after all, they are not doing anything. Just a bunch of smug fools praying. We will not be as tormented by its scorn as we are by the praise of the world for works of mercy, houses of hospitality and farming communes. They are necessary—they are the results of the work we are beginning. It is only by the grace of God they have sprung up and prospered.

A REFLECTION DURING THE SOLITARY RETREAT

I sit here on a clear cold winter's afternoon down on Long Island, surrounded by a snow-covered countryside, and listen to the Philharmonic Symphony. At the same time I darn stockings, three pair, all I possess, heavy cotton, gray, tan, and one brown wool, and reflect that these came to me from the cancerous poor, entering a hospital to die. For ten years I have worn stockings which an old lady, a dear friend, who is spending her declining years in this hospital, has collected for me and carefully darned and patched. Often these have come to me soiled, or with that heavy, hospital smell which never seemed to leave them, even after many washings. . . . But the fact remains that I have stockings to cover me when others go cold and naked.

The fact remains that I am now listening to a concert, Brahms' Second Symphony, joyful music to heal my sadness. All day I have felt sad. I am oppressed in general by a sense of failure, of sin. Abbot Marmion advised one of his penitents to cultivate a sense of compunction so I am indeed blessed in having this. The sins of my entire past life from earliest childhood come often to my mind to fill me with a sense of iniquity. St. Augustine was right when he talked of the wickedness there is even in children. One does not wonder then at the punishment that descends on the entire world . . . as a result of sin. I only regret that I do not have to suffer more of this punishment myself.

THE DESIRE FOR PENANCE (Another solitary retreat reflection)

The desire for penance is instinctive in every human heart. I think it is in the encyclical of Pius XI, quoted in the Breviary as one of the lessons for the feast of the Sacred Heart, that brings this out. One *desires* to share in the sufferings of Christ. One desires to share in the hardships of the beloved, hunger, thirst, vigils, and . . . [illegible]. That this can lead to Jansenism, Catharism, Individualism, is the charge of some priests when one talks of penance, mortification, detachment from creatures. But it is *love* that gives these desires and love is a glowing, happy thing, a radiant, warming fire. We want to strip ourselves to clothe our beloved. We want to fast because of his hunger, even if we cannot feed him, since we cannot feed the hungry of

India, China, Europe—we will share his sufferings and rejoice in this cross.

This blindness of love, this folly of love—this seeing Christ in others, everywhere, and not seeing the ugly, the obvious, the dirty, the sinful—this means we do not see the faults of others—only our own. We see only Christ in them. We have eyes only for our beloved, ears for His voice.

This is what caused the saints to go to what writers like Aldous Huxley (not to speak of our own Catholics) called repulsive extremes. "Always bearing about in our body the mortification of Jesus that the life also of Jesus may be made manifest in our bodies." 2 Cor. 4. 10.

Perhaps hagiographers were too prone to wallow in vomit, pus, sputum—the utterly repulsive—all to make their "point," as Peter would say, showing how the saints rose *above* the natural, the human, and became supernatural, superhuman, in their love. Nothing was difficult to them; all was clear, shining and beautiful on the pathway of love.

A REFLECTION, WRITTEN AFTER THE SOLITARY RETREAT

Every Friday afternoon I walked the mile to the village and took the train, getting off a few stops along the line and then walking another mile or so [to see her mother, Grace Day] and then sat and sewed and chatted with her. I'm so happy I had those hours with her now that she is dead. It is wonderful how after abandoning home and parents during the twenties one returns to them with love and appreciation during the forties.

But most of the week, those seven long days, I was alone. I got up at 6.30 for a seven o'clock Mass. The sisters, of course, were already in the chapel for their meditation and morning prayers. Then after a solitary breakfast, the only

meal I enjoyed during the day, I returned to the chapel for
another two hours of praying and meditative reading.

During the month of October I read St. Teresa's [of
Avila] treatises on prayer, or some of them. Mostly I labored at watering the garden of my soul, with much toil.
The litanies, the rosary, repetitive prayer always helped to
put me in an attitude of adoration and thanksgiving and
petition.

Sometimes I prayed with joy and delight. Other times
each bead of my rosary was heavy as lead. My steps
dragged, my lips were numb. I felt a dead weight. I could
do nothing but make an act of will and sit or kneel, and
sigh in an agony of boredom. Taking refuge in St. Bene-
dict's advice to pray often and in short prayers I took flight
on these occasions and walked, or went back to my room
and read or tried to work. I well discovered what acedia
was, that noonday devil, so well described in Helen Wad-
dell's translation of *The Desert Fathers.*

In the afternoon I tried to rest but restlessness was often
my portion. I read also two hours daily on Goodier's *Life
of Jesus Christ,* which I have found unequalled. . . .

I came to the conclusion during those months that such
a hermit's life for a woman was impossible. Man is not
meant to live alone. . . . To cook for one's self, to eat by
one's self, to sew, wash, clean for one's self is a sterile joy.
Community, whether of the family, or convent, or boarding
house, is absolutely necessary. . . .

From that "year" I spent away from my work, I began to
understand the greatness of the Little Flower [St. Thérèse
of Lisieux]. By doing nothing she did everything. She let
loose powers, consolations, a stream of faith, hope and love
that will never cease to flow. How much richer we are
because of her. . . .

My daughter will be married in April.

After her solitary retreat, Dorothy returned to her "community,"
the Mott Street house of hospitality, and, aside from her travelings, it
was with the Worker community that she remained for the rest of

her life. There, somehow, amidst the pressures, the "incidents," and the disruptions, she persevered in her reach for sanctity. Prayer was the vital and sustaining part of her spiritual life.

A "MOST CERTAIN UNDERSTANDING" (Notes. December 16, 1958)

Yesterday morning I woke with the most certain understanding that all in this life is merely a preparation for the next—a practice, a study, to pass our exams. Also a sense of the real work of that hour of prayer, that feat of endurance, that hour in the desert, that hour of suffering that the Little Sisters make that Our Lord can transform so easily into joy.

PRAYER AND SANCTITY

The purpose of prayer is to ask for grace, to let Christ grow in us. Prayer comes first. The reason we have so few saints is because we have not asked.

THE COMFORT OF PRAYER (Notes. February 13. Ca. the sixties)

Pouring rain today. I stayed in, resting—feeling exhausted. Sorrow, grief, exhaust one. Then tonight the prayers, the rosaries I've been saying were answered. And the feeling that prayers are indeed answered when we cry out for help was a comfort in itself. I had the assurance that they were answered tho it might not be *now*. I would not perhaps see the results. "Praised be God, the God of all consolation. He comforts us in all our afflictions and enables us to comfort those who are in trouble with the same consolation we have had from him." 1 Cor. 1.3–7.

Suffering drives us to prayer and we are comforted. Or at least strengthened to continue in faith, and hope, and love.

PRAYING FOR THE WORLD

We are praying constantly, but for the world.

THE NECESSITY FOR PRAYER

St. Teresa calls prayer a "violence" and says that those who spend at least two hours daily are rewarded by increased strength to combat the world. We can do nothing without prayer. We go backwards when we stop praying. . . . We must pray as regularly as we eat in order to grow.

We must pray with humility and with confidence. We are nothing without Him. We can do nothing, not even lead a natural life. We depend, every moment, on God. . . .

Pray with confidence. Ask and *you shall receive.* That is a condition laid down by God. God does not lie. Ask for love. Ask for grace. Even at moments of sin. God answers always.

DOROTHY'S ADVICE TO A LONELY PERSON (N.d. Dorothy copied and saved this letter.)

We all want someone to lean on and we all feel alone and we all rebel against freedom and responsibility. We always will. But we just have to take it. The only remedy is prayer and usually we will put off that and look for someone to lean on and give us comfort. We might as well make up our minds that we are not going to find it. We may think we find it but such support crumbles under us.

You can depend on nobody but God and yourself. It is a hard enough fight controlling oneself without trying to control others. I always feel that we should expect everything from people—"they are a little less than angels"—and then on the other hand, be surprised or disappointed about nothing, remembering "they are but dust."

A PRAYER IN JAIL AND A REFLECTION ON COMMUNITY (Notes. July 12, 1957)

The prison experience to which Dorothy refers is that of 1956 following her and her friends' refusal to take cover during an air raid warning alert.

No sooner did I take my rosary in my hands and . . . [illegible] the lights out, that I felt a sense of such closeness to God. Such a sense of His love, such love for His creatures. . . .

I was wondering if I would have had this strong sense alone. Being with others, sharing with others, makes the Cross so much easier. God has provided a natural way to Heaven, generally speaking. A mother with her children does not suffer the tormenting desires—the little foxes. Walking with others the pains of fatigue are lessened. Suffering cold with others—a blanket seems to wrap one and all. . . .

PRAYER AND SAINTHOOD

The purpose of prayer is to ask for grace, to let Christ grow in us. Prayer comes first. The reason we have so few saints is because we have not asked. The reason we do not have sanctity is because we do not ask. Prayer has the power to take you to sanctity.

The intention of the prayer is primary. If we pray for our sanctification so that we may glorify God it is never refused. To pray for all other things, like health, a job, to avoid danger, may be refused. But they are refused only if they do not promote God's glory. If it fits in with our sanctification it will be given to us.

We pray to bring the life of Christ into our own life, into our own time. We are asking for the Cross, for suffering. Suffering is to surrender our own will.

Pray always, that our whole life is used to promote God's glory and to loving Christ in others. If you keep on praying you will become a saint. If we do not become holy, it is our own fault.

HOW TO PRAY (A retreat conference note. Staten Island farm, January 28, 1951)

Prayer is an effect of love. If you love you pray. Prayer is raising our hearts and minds. As humans we have two great faculties—mind and will. Prayer is not a short mumbling of words. It is not directed toward self as an outlet for our feelings. It must be an effort to contact God. We may find it hard, dry or cold, but the effort must be there. St. Thomas says unless distractions are deliberate they in no way lessen the merit or efficacy of the prayer. There is only one thing that distractions will take from you: the consolations, refreshment, and rest of prayer. But these are not the most important.

Prayer has to be doctrinal. Not sentimental, subjective. Good will is not enough. It has to have good sense.

FATHER HUGO ADVISES DOROTHY ON PRAYER (Letter. N.d.)

If your prayer is an ordeal, giving you no sensible consolation, but seeming to be a waste of time and even a subtle hypocrisy—this is all the better. For then you are praying by faith and not by sense. And prayer is always a weariness to the natural man.

A PRAYER BY DOROTHY (Sunday, June 19, 1955)

Light up in our hearts the light of the divine knowledge of Thee, O Lord, Who lovest mankind, and openest the eyes of our souls to the understanding of the teachings of Thy Gospel. Instill in us the fear of Thy blessed commandments, so that trampling upon earthly desires we may come to a spiritual life, thinking and performing all things according to Thy will. For Thou art the light of our souls and bodies, O Christ, our God, and we give Thee Glory, together with Thy eternal Father and Thy most holy blessed and lifegiving spirit, now and forever. Amen.

8

Perseverance

Perseverance is the companion to conversion, since conversion is never completed in time.

LOVE AND SPIRITUAL PROGRESS (Notes. April 28, 1953)

> Love requires *constant* struggle. The less we work at love, the colder we become and the harder it is to receive the warmth of God's love. Religion is not just thinking—it is love. We shall be pierced.

CONSTANCY AND FIDELITY (Fall "Appeal," 1974)

> It is 4.30 and time for an hour in our parish church around the corner. The Mass is at 5.30 p.m., and strength and courage to endure will come with the Mass. News came last night of my oldest granddaughter, Becky, bearing her second child, a boy. I wish one of my grand-children would name a child either Fidel (!) or Constance, since these names indicate the virtues I most admire—Fidelity and Constancy.

A NEW DAY

Every day sees us making a new start. It seems the old man will never die, the new never born. . . . A saint can make a morning offering—saints always renewed their intention to please God.

THE PAIN OF NIGHT (Notes. N.d.)

My nights are always in sadness and desolation and it seems as tho as soon as I lie down I am on a tack of bitterness and pain. Then in the day I am again strong enough to make an act of faith and love and go on in peace and joy.

NO RESTING POINT IN THE LIFE OF THE SPIRIT

When a person says he has done enough he has already perished. Some movement is always necessary—forward or backward. There is no vacation in the spiritual life.

A SELF-EXAMINATION (Notes. March 29, 1951)

This afternoon, glimpses of my own ugliness, vanity, pride, cruelty, contempt of others, levity, jeering, carping. Too sensitive to criticism, showing self-seeking love.

PERSEVERANCE IN A VOCATION

The Magi faithfully fulfilled their vocation. They have been ridiculed by people for following a star and looking for a King. The Magi were astronomers, putting their science to good use. Some of the saints seemed to have had the same disposition toward searching the heavens—St. Ignatius used to stand on a balcony to scan the heavens; St. Francis stood on a mount. We are too busy to rest ourselves in contemplating the harmony of creation. We need solitude and silence to look up to God. The Magi did. We, like the Magi, should follow the light of faith, seeking God alone.

FINAL PERSEVERANCE

We are not sure of final perseverance. The objective is not a burden but a privilege.

PERSEVERANCE

Perseverance is the greatest of all virtues.

PROGRESS. LOAVES AND FISHES (Ms. 184)

Sometimes it takes but one step. We would like to think so. And yet the older I get the more I see that life is made up of many steps, and they are very small affairs, not giant strides.

9

Scripture

The Bible was one of the first of the foundation elements on which Dorothy built her structure of faith. Perhaps it was from her "atheist" father (who always carried a Bible on his person) that as a child she acquired some sense of the particular sacredness of the book. Another source of this feeling was the Methodist services she, as a child, attended with a friend when the family lived in California. That the Lacouture retreat placed a direct emphasis on the Bible for the truths it sought to teach was, in Dorothy's view, one important reason for the retreat's effectiveness.

THE GOSPEL AND THE RETREAT (From an undated handwritten note)

A popular and friendly cardinal on the East Coast told me once that he "didn't think much" of that group of ours. . . . Who do they think they are, saying compline together? A bunch of priests?

And as for reading the Scriptures, it was indeed true that permission had to be obtained in the Carmelite convents in France to read various parts of the Old Testament. One of the Sisters of Thérèse of Lisieux copied out a good part of the Old Testament to read, a work of love and devotion. Many a priest I have met feel the layman is going beyond his rights to read the various translations of Scripture which have not had the Imprimatur of the Church.

Actually I think to myself with a touch of bitterness that the ordinary man does not hear the Word of God. . . . Never have I heard it as I hear it now, each year in retreat, and with the sureness that it is indeed the Gospel. The average Catholic is baptized, instructed for his first holy communion, then confirmation, and then, Sunday after Sunday, the short Masses repeat themselves with inadequate sermons, all the announcements, appeals for money. The shepherds are not feeding their sheep. But they themselves have not been fed. . . .

And the sad part is, the people are poor, and do not know they are poor. Poor, undernourished, and even starving, as far as spiritual nourishment goes.

THE BIBLE AS AN ACCOUNT OF GOD'S LOVE FOR HUMANKIND

The Church is very insistent that we read the Bible, especially the New Testament. Saint Jerome says that he who does not know the New Testament does not know Christ. Saint John Chrysostom: "The Mind of Paul is the mind of Christ." Father [Louis] Farina says that the New Testament is a love letter from the Holy Spirit to us. The more we read the Bible the more we grow in love.

PRAYING THE PSALMS ("Acceptance Speech," August 8, 1968. Liturgical Movement Conference, St. John's Abbey, Collegeville, Minnesota)

It was the liturgy which led us to praying the psalms with the Church, leading us to an understanding joy in prayer. I remember Father Paul Hanley Furfey [a sociologist at

Catholic University] saying to us, "if you just say the three psalms a night, the twenty-one psalms a week, which make up the Compline psalms, you will soon have twenty-one psalms which keep coming to mind in times of stress." And certainly that has been true.

It was the liturgy which brought us close to scripture with all the new translations, the New Standard Version, the Knox translation, the Phillips paraphrase (I have heard it called) and now the Jerusalem Bible, with all its notes and commentaries. The "hard sayings" of the Gospel became for us truly a sword which pierced the heart and separated us often from family and friends.

SCRIPTURE AND REDEMPTION

The best thing to do in the cause of our redemption and real freedom is to read the Scriptures. Then read what the canonized saints have to say.

10

The Jews

From the history of any phenomenon there is derived some understanding of its character in terms of those cause-effect patterns which
historians build to justify their work. So it is with the Jews, except,
like existence itself, one begins with mystery. Why the Creator
should have chosen this nomadic and warlike people is a mystery.
Why should He not have preferred the Sumerians, or the Egyptians,
for example, as the people to whom He revealed His reality and His
laws for a life that would be pleasing to Him? Given the character of
Jewish life during that early period, it is not a mystery that He, who
seemed to have rendered His utterances in manlike tones, was referred to as "He." Nor is it a mystery that in the Old Testament
narrations He should have so frequently been cast into the role of a
warrior who directed armies and won stunning victories.

The mystery, however, continues in that once "chosen," the mark
of that event is still at work in the life of the Jews. Down through the
centuries of their testing, frequently so cruel, these Job-like sons and
daughters of Abraham have struggled to remain faithful to the Covenant that Yahweh made "in perpetuity" with Abraham, their father.
It was a Covenant made with a people, a community, and as a community the Jews, a minority people far-flung to many lands, have
survived every sociological factor that would have made them only a
faint memory in the lands they inhabited.

The mystery is magnified before the fact that those who have lived
by the Covenant with Abraham have carried in their lives the burden
of oppression and violence inflicted upon them because they had

about them the sign of an impenetrable "otherness." The fear that comes from this sign has roots that go into a fathomless darkness and there in the depths takes its nourishment from the blackness around it. It is a fear not confined to any one people or nation, one with an eruptive potential which, one is inclined to think, is beyond bringing to light through historical analysis and then extirpating it, since the fear comes from a source beyond the reach of "objective criteria."

It is a fear that trails into a curious design, since the suffering which has been so much the part of Jewish life has occurred at the hands of those whose association has been with a culture and past called "Christian."

In Jesus, a Jew of the line of David, born to the simplest and humblest in the society about him, the Covenant with Abraham was given a new dimension. The Old Law stood, changed not by one "jot or tittle," but was crowned with the law of love. It was inherent in the divine unity of love itself that the New Covenant should be for all —all who had ever been or ever would be.

The responsibility for the desolation of the Jews is in the failure of Christians to be faithful to Christ's new commandment. Inasmuch as Christ's law of love flowed out of the Covenant with Abraham, that law should have become the mark of the community of Christendom, as the first Covenant had become the mark of the community of the Jews. And the Jews then would have had a special place of honor in the history of the world and even an organic connection with their prophet, Christ, because they gave humankind the foundation on which the community of peace could be built. They would be further honored for their example of making their Covenant with Abraham an instrument that raised the particularity of self to the richness of community, the community of all who would stand against all the desecrations that history might lay upon it.

But Christian culture never produced a community sense of cherishing the Jews for their special offering to its life, nor has it produced a community sense of the transcendent value of peace. The love of which Christ taught has been seen as changing the lives of persons who then, usually, are set aside from the business of history. This attitude that the work of love is effected in persons who are exceptional and who otherwise can be dismissed is one that has produced a deformation of the Body of Christ.

No two people stand more in the light of seeing the special place of the Jews in divine history than Peter Maurin and Dorothy Day. Neither, of course, stood alone. In the thirties the French personalists, especially Jacques Maritain, recognized the hideousness of the maelstrom of anti-Semitism that was forming, and no one has written a more passionate denunciation of anti-Semitism from the Christian standpoint than that found in Léon Bloy's essay, "Israel," in his *The Pilgrim of the Absolute.* Bloy was contemporary to Maurin, and Maurin was thoroughly familiar with his works.

As World War II approached, Maurin wrote a series of brief essays for the *Catholic Worker* under the general heading of "Save the Jews for Christ's Sake." His plea was that America should give hospitality without stint to all Jews seeking to escape the murderous oppression then developing. Maurin called them an "imperishable people," and he acutely recognized the inseparable character of Judaism and Christianity where the life of the latter was concerned.

Maurin wanted to "Judaize" Christianity. He would have all who professed the community of Christ take on their own characterizing mark, not as members of a class or nation, primarily, but as members of the Body of Christ. He wanted the Christian community to give the world a new air to breathe, a new climate—one of peace and a generous sharing of the world's goods with those in want. The spirit of Christ, he believed, should be manifested in more than persons acquiring safe-conduct passes to heaven. It should renew the earth.

All that Peter affirmed, Dorothy affirmed, and on no point more certainly than on the Jews, as some of her thoughts indicate.

RANDOM REFLECTIONS (The *Catholic Worker,* October-November 1978)

"Happy the people the Lord has chosen for His own." The Jews are indeed God's chosen, and *God does not change.* I read a long interview with Chaim Potok. My heart warms to him. His books are all beautiful, bringing to my mind the high esteem in which Jewish men hold their wives, mothers of their households.

Watched a documentary on television, "The Chosen People" with Elie Wiesel. (I am reading his book *Night.)*

To have lived through the Fr. Coughlin era is indeed to have seen something of the persecution of God's chosen. [A certain Monsignor] . . . wanted to buy the *Catholic Worker* for $2,000. Naturally we refused. To Fr. Coughlin's credit, he did, with the contribution of his immense following, build a great number of rural churches in the deep South, which I came across on my speaking trips around the country. But his talk of international Jewish bankers stirred up a wave of anti-Semitism.

A VISIT TO A JEWISH TABERNACLE (Notes. 1956)

In the back yard of an old tenement on Pitt Street, across from Our Lady of Sorrows Church . . . a young Jew in a doorway . . . took us thru the long narrow green painted passage to a very small dingy back yard, and there, built on one side of cinder blocks and roofed with bamboo (sometimes it is just branches of trees) there was this shelter, with tables and benches, lanterns hanging, prayers on the walls. The orthodox Jews eat and sleep here thru these days of the Feast of the Tabernacle. The command to keep this feast is in Leviticus and Catholics read this as a lesson in the Mass of one of the September Ember Days.

THE MEANING OF THE SYNAGOGUE FOR CHRISTIANITY

The value of the synagogue is derived from Christ. The synagogue led up to Him. He is the center. Jesus is hidden in the Old Testament. His presence sanctified the Old Law which contained Him. Christ puts His seal on the Old Tes-

tament in the presence of John, the last voice of the Old
Testament. John is the last of the prophets. That work is
continued in the Church through faith. The Church now
bears children by faith. The Church is Mary, the Spouse of
Christ. So Christ carries on the work.

FINDING THE MESSIAH IN THE JEWS (Easter Wednesday, 1972)

I began to know the Jewish people then, [when she began
to work for the Socialist *Call* in 1917] in the breaking of
bread as I was later to know Christ. I began to "go with"
Mike Gold not long after, and when he wrote a play "On
the Airshaft" (his mother's apartment on Chrystie Street
had rooms on the airshaft common to tenement apartments) I used to go with him to the Provincetown Playhouse on Macdougal St. in Greenwich Village and often
since have been called a Villager. But I despised the arty
atmosphere, the liberal mind, as opposed to the radical,
and always associated myself, then and now, with the
Lower East Side. . . . I was steeped in it and still am.

Elie Wiesel brings back to me that feeling of joy and
sadness of [that time]. I found the Messiah in the Jew. One
might say living there brought my conversion to Catholicism closer.

"SALVATION IS FROM THE JEWS"

"Salvation is from the Jews," St. Paul said. . . . In them,
thru them, I am always finding the Messiah. The sayings of
the Hasidic fathers have often saved me from despair. Like
that saying Elie Wiesel quotes in *Souls on Fire:* "I am much
more afraid of my good deeds that please me than of my
bad deeds that repel me."

A LESSON FROM THE EGYPTIAN EXILE

The story of the chosen people shows what God will do for souls. They were in Egypt for 430 years of exile. After long and persevering prayer, God, thru Moses, led them out.

TO BE A JEW (Note. 1952)

To be a Jew—singled out—a priestly people—unique—to be a Jew is something sacramental.

THE JEWS AND THE INFANT CHURCH (Notes. December 17, 1947, at her sister Della's house)

And now it is with great joy that I read in Fr. [John] Oesterreicher's booklet another explanation of "Salvation is from the Jews." . . . He quotes Msgr. Chas. Jourmet as saying of the infant Church, "Never again on earth will the Church be so fervent, so loving, so pure as when she was wholly Jewish. Never again in the course of the ages will she find sanctity like that of the Blessed Virgin or even like that of the Apostles." St. Augustine wrote in wonder that "it has not been recorded that any Church or pagan nations did this" [its members selling all that they had to provide for all].

11

The Pain and Pleasure of Retreats

Dorothy's quest for sanctity never brought her to the point where she acquired that final coat of the varnish of sweet piety which in old tales was the mark of the finished saint. She remained the essential Dorothy. She could be acidulous, harsh, and cutting, but invariably her final word on a person or situation was based on compassion and understanding.

ALCOHOL (Notes)

Dorothy's dislike of "drink" was near absolute. She saw little about it that was humanizing, socializing, or even tolerable. One of the unhealed wounds which she carried with her through her days was Malcolm Cowley's remark in his *Exile's Return* that she, as a Village bohemian, could, drink for drink, match the capacity of any burly stevedore. She denied it; she denied it for the rest of her life; she denied that she was a "hidden" alcoholic or that she suppressed a need for it by smothering it with religion. She might have saved her energy because most people recognized the humor in Cowley's exaggeration. She found alcohol intolerable because it distorted the reality that she would meet head on. Then too, she was continually affronted by its ravaging effect on the lives of people that clung to her for support. It seemed almost that everywhere she turned at the Worker houses of hospitality she was confronted by people who were dehumanized by alcohol.

At the time of the Newburgh retreat alcoholic priests had become a particular problem.

> The last time I was up here the problems with drink were as usual. John is always drinking a little, a bad example, and certainly aging him. . . . [As to the alcoholic priests] I worry that I do not give them enough attention and yet each one would absorb you completely—your time and energy, if you would let them. And now Fr. A. He believes he is persecuted by Mabel and George. He writes bitter sarcastic letters to Tim, inviting him to psychoanalyze him.

THE BEGINNING OF A RETREAT AND THE WAYS OF THE LORD (Notes. September 1946)

> Sunday. The Feast of the Seven Sorrows of the Blessed Virgin Mary. The priest to give the retreat showed up with a heavy smell of liquor on his breath. Perhaps he had a cold. "The ways of the Lord are unscrupulous."

ALCOHOL AND VIOLENCE (Part of the atmosphere of a funeral and a retreat at Tivoli, New York, June 1966. Notes. Tuesday, June 17, 1966)

> Joe Cotter died on the way to the hospital. He had emphysema. [The day of the funeral, June 22.] Some of the mourners [under the influence] are accusing others of no grief . . . there is violence. . . . The hardest thing to bear is when [they] . . . glorify their drinking as "being with the poor, the sinner."

This was the only instance of the intrusion of spirits (intoxicating) into the atmosphere of a retreat, but there were annoyances and exasperations to be suffered.

THE PAIN OF WEARINESS DURING A LONG RETREAT DISCOURSE

Meanwhile I listen as tho fixed to the Cross, aching, stiffening, while Elias travels from Carmel to Sinai, fleeing, while Matthew jumps up from his tax table (the kind Jesus overturned perhaps) and prepared a banquet, a farewell to his past life, a feast for Jesus, an invitation accepted. And Peter fished, and jumped into the sea from the constraint of the boat, and Zaccheus climbed a tree! . . .

Retreats are hard.

AN UNBEARABLE RETREAT CONFERENCE

I have ceased to try to listen. It is so irritating. I can only think, at any rate we are sitting in the presence of the Blessed Sacrament. Patience, patience, which means suffering. Such very bad delivery, so many mumbled words—jumbled up—that he is very difficult to listen to. It is very technical theologically—hard for the men who sit patiently —God bless them.

THE WANDERING MIND (Notes. N.d.)

My mind . . . goes to the volume of letters which they wrote from jail [Sacco and Vanzetti] which Bob has now. I had found it being used as a door stop, wedged under a door to hold it open—all battered by wind and rain! And my St. John of the Cross left out under an apple tree—rain-soaked too. And my Halgren's catechism stolen. I know by whom because he thought I, aspiring to be poor, must be kept poor. My autographed Maritain—Eric Gill!

DOROTHY PASSES A NOTE

What is the matter with the Jones girl sitting next to Arthur Lacey? Is she having a breakdown or something? Has she acted this way before?

Answer: Mother noticed this sort of motion in church.

A RETREAT EVE DISTURBANCE (Note. N.d.)

As usual before a retreat or day of recollection all hell broke loose. Karen and Sue fighting in the night—guests arrived Saturday night. More scenes. Julia up all night because she had to give up her attic to the men. Linda is sleeping in the dining room.

Thank God we can have conferences in the chapel. The first fifteen minutes were interrupted by the cow mooing.

A CASE OF NERVES (Notes. July 1948)

This morning between conferences I wept, partly for joy, partly for the misery of life, partly in self-pity at being so overwhelmed, partly thru fatigue and nerves.

For instance. During the second conference one of "the friends of the family" came in, stood in the back, sat down, got up, sat down again. Again at the rosary, the chapel was crowded, so he together with a half dozen others knelt in the conference room, and he chose a huge overstuffed chair to kneel before. Bending over it, he buried his face in the depths of the upholstery. There was sensuality in the gesture, pathology, even.

OH COMMUNITY! A RETREAT-TIME MEAL

Frances said it was sacrilegious to read the story of the Last Supper while we feasted. When she ran out of the room I don't know whether it was to weep or blow her nose. . . . But she ate heartily, much meat. She was very much upset because the children ate her 2 slices of protein bread.

Oh community! as Betty says.

A COMPLAINT AND THEN SHAME (Notes. N.d.)

It is a very close still day. Very silent. Only an occasional song of a bird. These days are very hard. I am so used to being the Martha. It is the fifth day of an eight-day retreat and I have never made so long a one before. The silence, the not doing anything would not be so hard if it were not attended by so many small physical discomforts. Such as glasses which do not fit properly, always sliding down one's nose. A pew in the chapel made for very short people and straight-backed. I am jackknifed into it. A too tight girdle, made more tight by my own slackness—due to lack of exercise. Too short and too tight stockings (a donation to the poor). Occasional hot flashes, even at my age—61. Pains in the back, in hips, knees. St. Teresa of Avila says one should be comfortable at prayer!

And here among us eight, there is Dixie, a prisoner for many years in her bed, lying on a hard rented stretcher, wheeled in and out of the chapel, condemned to a life of immobility, a constant example to us of uncomplaining endurance and sweetness and patience, and of vigorous intel-

lectual life. All of which adds to my shame at my own lack
of endurance. God forgive me.

There were the good moments of repose and even delight during
retreat periods and Dorothy recorded these too.

A MOMENT OF REPOSE (Notes. Easton. Summer 1943)

It is half past five, just past benediction. I should be walking but it is very close and my head aches a little so here I
sit near the statue of St. Anthony by the flowerbed. There
are two large fat robins and three smaller ones. There are
two woodpeckers bigger still with very long bills. There are
three tiny little birds, so small the grass almost hides them.
A chipmunk runs across the grass and a little rabbit,
scarcely bigger than the woodpecker, races across the lawn
to stand posed *[sic]* under a fir tree. He is there a long time
until someone coming along frightens him and he scurries
into the flowerbed. A typical St. Anthony scene.

Inside the main house there is the sound of setting tables,
the happy sound of children's voices. Outside, a puppy
barking, small chirrupings from the birds, and now a train
in the distance. The world in one sense is very far away. We
have gone up on a high hill apart to be taught.

What a love of natural beauty that poor man, St. Francis,
had. The first thing he did in the beginning of his spiritual
life was to clean up and rebuild a church. It was he who
thought of having reenacted for us every Christmas that
scene in the stable so now we have our crèches, our "crib
sets," as we call them.

We have had supper, soup, bean and lettuce salad, meat-
balls, fruit and coffee. Afterwards I made the stations of the
Cross. . . . Then I took a walk saying the rosary. While
walking I picked some sweet clover which is in the back of
my notebook now. And as I write, sitting here at my desk
in the conference room, little bugs make exploratory trips
around the desk and a measuring worm paces out its way

across the back of the desk. Not content with what it is finding, it has made its way back to my bunch of weeds, my sweetgrass, which is as good a sample as I know of God's sweetness.

Father Hugo said once, quoting from somewhere, that the best thing to do with the best of things is to give them up. Well, I have long since "given up," "offered up," the field and the shore for the city slum. "Why are you staying here?" Father [Vincent] McNabb's friends asked him, he who was living in London but was forever talking about "Nazareth or social chaos." "To get people out of here," he replied.

So it is my vocation to agitate, to be a journalist, a pamphleteer, and now my time must be spent in these cities, these slums. But how wonderful it is to be out here in this Christian community, set in the midst of fields, atop a hill and to have samples of Heaven all about—not hell. I truly love sweet clover and thank God for it.

ANOTHER RETREAT SCENE (Notes. Newburgh. Summer 1954)

Oh the beauty of young people gathered together on a retreat, . . . sitting under trees, reading St. Augustine, St. Bernard, their missals and their Bibles.

Newman said the first need of a university in Greece was a grove of trees. Here at Maryfarm we wander between hedges of wild cherry making the stations, or out thru the fields under the great ancient oaks or sit under the maples and the pines watching the traffic which has all the fascination of movement, a flowing stream. . . .

There is the beauty of all the seasons on this land, on these farms which have been made beautiful and fruitful by hard work, the hard work of saints and sinners, and all the in-betweens.

STILL ANOTHER (Notes. Newburgh. Summer 1954)

During the retreat so many, I included, like to sit on the grassy lawn, under the Norway pines, by the highway and watch the continuous stream of traffic flow by. There is something soothing in the constant movement, like the flow of a river, loud, continuous, wavelike, and a comfort in a sense of the stability of oneself.

It is very hot. There is a hot wind. The birds are vocal, there are clothes, sheets, towels flapping on the line. Occasionally the cawing of a crow. Now John Filliger is changing the cow to another part of the field and hammering in the stake which holds her. We have no fences, and he stakes out the young bulls and the cow and a billy goat and a nanny. He loves his animals and they are well cared for.

Now the cicadas are making their winding up noises in the trees. No katydids yet. The Queen Anne's lace is most beautiful now. There are daisies and black-eyed susans in the fields, too. What an enchanting thing silence is. Everything at once invested in peace; women are enveloped in mystery and beauty with it. And what recollection in the soul—what a time to pray!

A RETREAT REMEMBRANCE OF PETER MAURIN (Notes. Newburgh. Friday, June 22, 1950)

This morning during the conference I looked out of the window to see a dove, a pigeon on the roof of the porch. Then later in the morning while we were in chapel, there it was under the crab apple tree, then in a cleft in the rock wall, then again it flew up to the roof of the cement-house, right over Peter's room, resting there, and aside from some hoppings and preenings, it stayed right there for a few hours. Ellen said she fed it—that it was a carrier pigeon.

THE JOY OF SILENCE (Notes. August 1948)

One of the great joys of this retreat is the silence, although there is, of course, plenty of noise—of traffic going by, of airplanes, of the kitchen, the homely sounds of the farm— chickens, cows. But the silence of people is wonderful. It is like balm upon a wound. The city has been so full of noise lately.

There has been the yearly festa of Mott Street, for the feast of the Assumption, Santa Assunta being the patron saint of the people of Bari, which is where the folks around Mott St. come from.

Every year for August 12–15 lights are strung elaborately in festoons and stars across the streets, stands for cooking pasta and pizza and broiled sausages and cheese pies and boiled corn and watermelon and roasted chickpeas are set up on the curb and since the streets are narrow and the sidewalks also, these stands have to be put up nightly.

Then there is the bandstand right across from our hospice, where each night there is not only a band concert, a vaudeville performance of Italian singers, romantic and comic, but a concert thru loudspeakers so that a whisper of one of the performers can be heard ten blocks away. One can imagine what the crescendo and climax of an anguished song about a broken heart is like. . . .

[Today I hear the] . . . shoutings and singings, of business, of play, of quarreling, of friendliness, . . . and magnified, multiplied—what gigantic gargantuan voices these are. They would fill the Metropolitan, the Yankee Stadium, Madison Square Garden, all combined. I lie in my bed and think of an immense field at night and I want to imagine lying in the middle of it, contemplating the heavens, and the silence.

Noise has been one of the things that oppresses me.

12

Grace and the Social Order

Dorothy was seventy-three years old when she wrote the following: "Yesterday was the beginning of the preparation for Lent and I will take as my Lenten stint, beginning now, the writing of this book, 'All is Grace.' The title really means 'all things work together for good to those who love God.' " Her profoundest conviction was that she was so a part of the soul of "all," that her own experience of grace should have the potential of an outward transmission until "all"—all of humankind and all of nature—should be touched. The light of grace was no slender shaft that rested upon her alone. She was a member of the Body of Christ—Christ, the Son of God, who had become a person and had entered into history—whose Body was not only the soul of the unity of Heaven but also of that potential of heavenly unity which existed in time.

On June 29, 1943, at the very height of World War II, and while Dorothy was saturating herself in the retreats, Pope Pius XII issued the encyclical *Mystici Corporis,* the Mystical Body of Christ, a document which affirmed that the communal, or social, life of grace was a true component of the totality of Christian grace. This encyclical provided an explicit Church declaration of the unity of all, seen and unseen. Coming, as it did, in the midst of war, it must have seemed to Dorothy that here was a statement of that final truth that transcended all the desolation, an explicit and direct affirmation by the Church of what Peter Maurin had taught her. It enabled her to quote with increased authority St. Catherine of Siena's phrase, "All the way to Heaven is Heaven." It was the work of the grace in her to clear the way to Heaven, to provide a new air and a new spirit in which the body of Christ might be magnified, in which the "all" that was potential might become actual.

The emphasis of the retreats was not, of course, on the social order. Their concern was with the life center of re-creation, the person. Still, some observations in "All is Grace" are concerned with society. To these, some other of her thoughts, taken from her later notes, have been added. In an era that waxes on an ever expanding complexity in all of its objects and social forms, Dorothy's social views may seem simplistic to the point of absurdity. Therein, perhaps, grace does shine.

The immediate social concern for Dorothy was the one at her doorstep, the poor. Providing for their need was one of the main works of her life.

JUDGING THE POOR

The poor often are poor all around. They can be poor in gratitude. But they are not put in our way to be judged, only that we may purchase heaven from them.

ATTITUDES TOWARD THE POOR (Notes. November 1951)

[Being judged] is perhaps the greatest burden the destitute have to bear: the contempt, the judgment of others. "If they would do this and this, they would get along better." "If they would think this way, the way I think, if they did as I do, they would not have this mental breakdown." There is always that assumption of superiority, of having in some way managed better, knowing better, than anyone else, in the attitude of those who help the poor. It is everywhere. It is among those who work in bureaus. It is in us who go to live with the poor and try to serve them. We intrude on them with our advice: "If you go to Mass each day. If you say your rosary; if you kept better hours; stopped drinking; choose some good work; build up in yourself a philosophy of work, of poverty!" Oh yes, we have many plans to help the poor. If we could only feed them, shelter them, clothe them without question, without assuming that we had all of the answers.

WORLD WAR II AND THE CONCERNS OF THE POOR

The bourgeois . . . fights for abstractions like freedom, democracy, because he has the material things of this life (which he is most fearful of being deprived of). The poor fight for bread, for increase in wages, for time to rest, for warmth, for privacy.

OUR OWN POVERTY

How often we invite Our Lord into worse places than the stable. We offer Him the dung of our natural affection for objects; we offer Him the straw of frivolity, the ox of stupidity, the ass of selfishness. So we must ask for forgiveness and faith for our mind, hope for our heart, and charity for our will.

THE POOR

I got an illumination today thinking of St. John the Baptist who was content to speak, scatter seed and did not look for results. God is able of these stones to raise up children of Abraham. Leave it to God to bring the increase.

POVERTY

It gives glory to God to choose poor instruments.

REMAKING THE SOCIAL ORDER (A reply to certain people who objected to the poor and the deranged staying at the community house and farm)

We feel and have always felt since the work started, that when we accepted a man in the group and gave him a bed, we were accepting him as one of a family, as a brother. It is hard to *remake* men. It is not a matter of a few months or even a few years. On the one hand, we have to change the social order in order that men might lead decent Christian lives, and on the other, we must remake men to remake the social order. Order cannot be imposed from above. . . . it is going to be a long, a slow, suffering process. But the more we suffer with it, the more we will learn. . . . [I]nfinite patience, suffering, is needed. And it is never-ending. Think of Lazarus at the Gate. Read "The Honest Thief" by Dostoyevsky. There is a great lesson of love here. . . .

As for getting rid of those who offend and taking in others one may as well understand that the new batch will be exactly the same as the last. You cut off the head of the tyrant and two others spring up.

MAKING A CHRISTIAN SOCIAL ORDER

We cannot make a Christian social order without Christians. It is impossible, save by heroic charity, to live in the present social order and be Christian.

THE PROFIT SYSTEM

The social order which depends on profits, which does not consider men's needs as to living space, food, is a bad social order and we must work "to make that kind of society where it is easier for men to be good."

NOT GETTING ORGANIZED

What we need is an interior organism, the life of Christ within us. But we are always thinking of organization, the life of the world about us.

SOCIAL REVOLUTIONS AND THE CHURCH (Notes. Ca. the seventies)

The struggle for change in the secular field goes with a struggle in the Church. . . . The lesser clergy [in Latin America], nearer the poor, accept revolution as inevitable, try to find concordances, a basis for agreement, believing that in the end nothing can prevail against the Church.

Meanwhile people are lost to the Church, to faith. It is part of our duty to save them, to think in terms of body and soul. Faith comes by hearing—the body *is* important. But what kind of a social order are we to have?

"What kind of a social order are we to have?" Dorothy asks the question but she gives no answer in terms of the usual formularies: a representative democracy, a dictatorship, or the communist state. She gives no answer because she believed that all the comprehensive political philosophies and systems in the Western world were, either by design or in the nature of their first concerns and programs, partners in the process of denuding life of the attributes of spirit. The national states had become god; they had established the principles around which life was organized; they could annihilate humankind and the creation that had sustained it, and such was their madness that the acquisition of the instruments of holocaust had become almost their first work.

She wanted an order which would transmit to all of life the grace-bearing light of God. She wanted a social order whose character was freedom, a freedom not defined in terms of elections and politics, but one that released the person from the tyranny of "systems" so that he or she might become genuinely creative according to gifts of mind and natural inclinations. She wanted a society whose corporate vision was raised to beauty, whose radiant energy was peace, whose structure opened life to the ideal of the completion of community—that final point of focus where "all is grace."

Dorothy regarded the all-enveloping and darkening shadow that the modern state cast over the human spirit as oppressive to a spiritual life.

WHERE SOCIAL RE-CREATION BEGINS

Seek first the Kingdom of Heaven. There are no utopias.

EDUCATION, CATHOLIC AND OTHERWISE

If Catholic schools are fitting children to lead the supernatural life, are they preparing them to earn their living in a Christian manner? Educational systems must be changed. . . . Where is the "correlation of the spiritual and material" in education?

MOVING PICTURES

Moving pictures are forming the mentality of future generations. Children and young people are getting the mind of the world. In peacetime it is pleasure, luxury, and sex. In war, the message is one of hate. A lot of what we get from films is a colossal sham, a fool's paradise.

If people lived in the country there would not be this occasion of sin for children. Their work would keep them from it. How can we become holy without the land?

THE SPIRITUAL ASPECT OF WORK (What the Mother of God did)

Our Blessed Mother had to learn to spin and weave, then she had to make the garments for Our Lord and St. Joseph. Mary of Agreda said they had only one set of garments and if they were handwoven, they would last a lifetime. But I doubt not that Our Lady, if she had an opportunity, sewed, spun or wove for the poor. Anna, the wife of Tobias, worked in a weaving factory to help out in their poverty. St. Bonaventure says Our Lady worked in Egypt to earn the family's daily bread because St. Joseph could not earn enough. I don't doubt it. It was all part of the humiliation of poverty for St. Joseph.

FOOD

We eat to have strength to serve God. If there are pleasures of taste . . . we should take them gratefully.

I'm sure the Blessed Mother did not neglect her family duties. I am sure St. Joseph provided a handsome board of beautiful wood which Mary kept scrubbed, perhaps waxed, and she who "with her bosom's milk didst feed her own creator, Lord most high," must have seen to it that suitable meals were served Him who was like unto us in all things save only sin.

I have been getting an idea as to what was eaten in those days by what is eaten now by people in the same region. . . . Perhaps there was, aside from feasts, a monotony of diet most of the time that we should get back to for the sake of simplifying our lives.

THE BEST CHANCE. WHERE?

Where is there the best chance for children today? On the land. Give them a taste for it by building up a little farm with sheep, goats, rabbits, chickens, bees, a cow, horses—a sample of everything. How much more real the Gospels would be then. Animals have their distinct individualities, they must be treated with respect and love. Newman wrote about animals as well as angels in his *Unseen World.* Children would understand so much more.

Believing, as she did, in a simple, voluntaristic social organization, Dorothy was obviously critical of any final, or near final, plan of social order. The ideal state where she was concerned was anarchism, but of a kind considerably different from the radical definition given it by the revolutionaries of the pre–World War I era.

ANARCHISM, DOROTHY'S VERSION

[She wanted an] anarchism based on love, not hate. Self-government rather than an imposed government. A recognition of the dignity and glory of our sonship with God and what it entails, what abilities it confers. A recognition of our capacities for work: physically, mentally, spiritually.

To expect everything of ourselves, with God's grace, and not to judge others. To measure ourselves as to what God wants of us, what talents He has given us to use and not to compare ourselves or judge ourselves by others, whether better or worse. In that way to stand alone in self-reliance. On the other hand, to be so free from dominating others or wanting to influence others as to (1) not judge (this seems to be folly, but it is the folly of the Cross; it is sowing one's judgment); (2) to serve all men, to obey all men, to wash the feet of all men in love, recognizing our common humanity—we are one flesh, as is said of husbands and wives and what love surpasses that love? To love our brothers because Jesus, Son of God, gave us a picture of that love in the story of the prodigal son. That is the kind of father we have. No judgment there. To reach finally the madness of love, deep, profound, as profligate in its way as the son's tawdry loves had been profligate.

The true anarchist asks nothing for himself. He is self-disciplined, self-denying, accepting the Cross without asking sympathy, without complaint.

The true anarchist loves his brother according to the new law, ready to die rather than *compel* his brother to go his totalitarian way, no matter how convinced he may be that his way is the only way.

CONSTRUCTIVE SOCIALISM

Dorothy's "anarchism" is obviously her formulation of a personal and social ideal. The social system that she seemed to have liked best was one outlined in Martin Buber's *Hasidic Axioms.*

According to Buber constructive socialism "becomes possible only through the formation of small voluntary groups of men who not merely share the means of production or the forces of labor, but who, as human beings, enter a direct relationship with one another and live a life of genuine fraternity. Such a socialism would have to resist any mechanization of living. The association of such groups would have to resist the dictates of an organized center, accumulation of power, and a 'political superstructure.' The focus of such groups, or cells, is not a political but a religious motivation."

THE COMMUNITY OF THE PARISH (A remembrance of Father Don Sturzo, written on August 10, 1959, following his death)

I have come to the farm [Peter Maurin Farm, Staten Island] to go thru the files for Don Sturzo's letters, mostly short messages. I must go to the library to get a list of his writings. . . . There will be much written about him. . . . How I wish I had been more faithful keeping a diary to write about such a man. Someone said he reminded them of the noble priest in Silone's *Bread and Wine,* but he never retired. He met each duty as it came, fearless, outspoken, understanding, trying to give guidance in the world of men. He was not one who thought in terms of how many "souls" there were in his parish. He thought of their needs, the kind of society suited to man and his freedom. I hope others will go and find out what kind of a village was his in Sicily, how the people lived—worked. How he came to take part in public affairs, start a cooperative, etc. . . .

He looked like that famous picture of Cardinal Newman, sitting, frail, dignified, scholarly, with noble, austere profile. Did Danilo Dolci know this valiant man—really know him with his heart and mind? Peter [Maurin] first told us of his work, of his writing—and when I mentioned his book, *Italy and the Fascismo,* at a college talk I gave, I was labeled a communist sympathizer because I was opposing Mussolini and his program. Then, as now, Catholic students were on the side of anyone opposing communism.

COMMUNISM (Notebook. December 17, 1947)

For years whenever I am asked at schools and colleges about the opposition between communism and Catholicism I have tried to be as simple as possible and quote from one of the *Queen's Work* pamphlets. There are three points [against communism]. The atheism, which is an integral part of Marxism, the use of violence to achieve social change, and the abolition of private property. And I like to quote Eric Gill who said "property is proper to man." But then, by the time I had pointed out our own use of force, our acceptance of modern war, our acceptance of a proletariat of those of another race or color, I had convinced my audience that not only was I opposed to finance capitalism, a capitalism founded on usury, but that I must still be a communist.

Trying to talk about these things is not so simple. . . . We who live on Mott St. have much to say on the necessity of property for the average man. When a family possesses nothing, and children are coming along, and there are old people to care for, one thinks longingly of a "house" rather than a flat, a home owned, not mortgaged, a plot of ground for fruit trees.

How can we teach our children about creation and a creator when there are only man-made streets about? How about life and death and resurrection unless they see the seed fall into the ground and die and yet bring forth fruit? A place to live, a home of one's own, 5 acres and liberty, 3 acres and a cow. And yet St. Gertrude said, "Property, the more common, the more holy it is." And Proudhomme said, "Property is theft."

Which reminds me of some religious orders. "Possessing nothing, yet possessing all things." It would sound like anti-clericalism to list the acreage of many monasteries in America, tax exempt, always extending, buying up farms and properties round about until entire villages are owned by an Order. "How much land does a man need?" How much land does an Order need, one might say. . . . But it does not seem becoming in an Order which has achieved the temporal security of ownership to deny private property for the masses, for the people who own nothing.

A DREAM ABOUT COMMUNISM (A note on N. K. Krupskaya's *Reminiscences of Lenin*. March 9, 1940)

Most of the 2nd volume which I have just finished reading is about a struggle between philosophies. I finished the book last night. I had been in bed sick with a headache all day which passed at nightfall. When I slept I dreamed of revolution and a poem, the last line of each stanza being, "Be kind, Cain!" It was almost in a tone of satire, directed at me. Helen [Iswolsky] said I was too kind to the Communists . . . and the attitude taken by our opponents is that we do not realize what they are capable of. Indeed we do! Revolution, terror, mob-spirit, makes murderers. But still in spite of the poem, our stand has to be "Love your enemies, overcome evil with good."

ATTENDING A COMMUNIST PARTY CONVENTION

"How can you go?" she was asked. (The *Catholic Worker*, March 1957)

I can only say, "I am a daughter of the Church," repeating the words of St. Teresa of Avila. It is as a daughter of the Church that I do these things. I might add, as a working journalist also, and the two are not in opposition.

THREE FORMS OF GOVERNMENT

This is a rough quotation, with which Dorothy agreed, from an unidentified source concerning three forms of government, "bourgeois liberalism, anti-individualistic communism, and fascist totalitarianism." (Note. December 22, 1950)

A final remark related to the attitude of these political philosophies toward Christianity. Of the three, the most irreligious is bourgeois liberalism. Christian in appearance, it has been atheistic in fact. Too skeptical to persecute, except for tangible profit, rather than defy religion, which it deemed an invention of the priesthood and gradually dispossessed by reason, it used it as a police force to watch over property.

THE FAILURE OF WESTERN DEMOCRACIES

The modern states which built up a Hitler [by the terms of the Versailles treaty], which did not depopulate concentration camps and gas chambers by giving asylum are monstrosities.

A PROPER ATTITUDE TOWARD AUTHORITY, WHATEVER THE SYSTEM (Notes. September 1953)

To see Christ in others, especially those in authority, as David saw . . . Saul, even when Saul kept trying to kill him. Even as Uriah did when he must have known the gossip of the Court. To see Christ and only Christ, even when following one's conscience, means what looks like defiance and disobedience. To guard the spirit in which one resists—the spirit of a child, combined with the judgment of a man. "To be subject to every living creature." We obey when we go to jail. Either register or go to jail. We are, after all, given a choice.

I'm afraid I have not kept this spirit of respect towards Senator McCarthy, [but still] there is no room for contempt of others in the Christian life. I speak and write so much better than I perform. But we can never lower the ideal because we fail in living up to it.

In every particular that related to the common good, Dorothy upheld the power of the government. To one particular, the ability of the state to make war, she absolutely dissented. She took exception to the fact that in the modern world the state had become the final focus of community and that the state, to preserve its life, had been given the ultimate right to assign to the possibility of death, if need be, the lives of its members. To Dorothy, the idea that the state could arrogate to itself the work of God by defining the "good" in its own terms, that it could kill in the interest of its presumed good, and, further, that it could place the entire human race in jeopardy by the power it possessed, was, as Dorothy would say, "monstrous."

NATIONALISM (Notes. Written during World War II)

Nationalism has been superseded by the dogma of the Mystical Body which is as old as Christianity. It is the mystery of Christ in us. . . . Because Jesus lives in you and me, we are one. This truth comes down from Heaven. We must try to grasp the reality that lies behind these words. In the conversion of St. Paul, one sentence contains this truth. "I am Christ whom thou persecutest." There is a real, vital, energizing union between the person and Jesus. We are one with Christ as Christ is one with the Father. *How*, is a mystery. When you think of Christ, think of the whole Christ, the fullness of Christ in space and time, a real existence. That the Mystical Body includes only Roman Catholics is heresy. The Mystical Body is the inseparable oneness of the human race from Adam to the last man. Can I have any animosity towards any Japanese, German, Italian —towards black or white? If we have animosity we are liars in Christ. There is no nationality. The only foreigner is he who has not Jesus in him and of human creation there never was such nor will ever be such. If men and women recognized this there would be no war.

RESISTING UNTO BLOOD. *But how?* (Notes. September 1942)

We are either at war or at peace. One of my comforts—that the sisters were still robing little girls for processions to scatter flowers before the Blessed Sacrament. Priests were still blessing the fields because people had to eat. And above all the great and kingly sacrifice of Christ our Lord, who laid down His life, who led a company of thousands upon thousands of martyrs—still goes on, all over the world. . . .

Belloc says Pascal is famous for the saying, "You have nothing to lose by the faith and nothing to gain." So I say the same of wars. We [of the human race] who are about to die anyway, as women, children, civilians—we have a right to cry out that we will die with the proper motive, of dying for our faith . . . for our belief in our fellows. We pray we will be able to die and that we will not be tormented and tortured. . . . And so I say too, we are going to be poor anyway—we are going to be unemployed anyway, we are going to die anyway, so let us revolt [against war].

FIGHTING FOR FREEDOM (Notes, N.d.)

I do not believe people can fight with *love*, with *charity*. Fighting is the expression of a denial of freedom, not a

working for it. To fight for freedom is only forging new
chains, exchanging old chains for new. God wants men to
be free, to love him and serve him in free choice. The whole
doctrine of freedom explains, to my satisfaction, at least,
the mystery of iniquity, the problem of evil in the world.

A PLAN FOR PEACE (Notes. N.d.)

Our only shelter these days is in Gethsemane. It is not in
resistance but in endurance. This is what the Holy Father
keeps telling us. The plan for peace is in the Scriptures, the
church, the confessional, the altar rail. We must begin ourselves and not blame those who don't know. We must have
peace at home first.

DETACHMENT

Detachment gives peace. Attachment gives war.

"HOW INVOLVED WE ALL ARE" (Notes. Ca. the seventies)

How involved we all are, with the hidden taxes we pay for
war, even when we make the gesture of refusing to pay
income tax, so much of which is used to finance wars.

We are all exploiters, as Orwell writes in one of his essays. Workers who consider themselves exploited are in fact
the exploiters of others. I remembered the general strike in
Belgium when the workers revolted against the austerity
regime brought about by the loss, or the giving up of the
African colony, the Belgian Congo.

. . . I thought—Garibaldi served the Church well when

he fought against the Papal States and relieved the Church
. . . of [the burden of administering them].

THE OBLIGATION OF OBEDIENCE—ONLY TO THE STATE (Notes. October 21, 1966)

Staying in bed for a day. Reading Simone Weil's essays.
Very interesting on Languedoc. Civilization. Also her ideas
on obedience. The concept is lost. There is no obligation of
obedience left except to the state.

Must get the entire score of Wagner's *Ring* from second-
hand store on Second Avenue. They have old librettos. Simone Weil likes Wagner. Karl Stern does not.

FOLLOWING THE SAINTS—BUT SOMETIMES NOT ALL THE WAY (Notes. August 20, 1953)

On St. Bernard preaching a crusade. And St. Francis
preaching peace. Men usually are of their time. St. Francis
is timeless. T. S. Eliot wrote in *Murder in the Cathedral*
that the greatest of all treasons was to do the right thing for
the wrong reason. They did the wrong thing for the right
reason. They all had the right reason—the glory of God.
We do not have to follow the saints blindly. Newman
whom we all dearly love and who is so close to us, who
writes so sublimely in his historical essays, wrote like any
insular Englishman of the Turk, the Hun, the Mongol. He
wrote as tho' they were scarcely men, scarcely capable of
conversion, the way so many in the Catholic press write of
the Communist. . . .

When as a pacifist I am asked, "What about the cru-
sades?" I must humbly reply, first that I only answer because St. Peter says we must give a reason for the faith that
is in us, and then, that it is hard to see that we gained much

by them. The Middle East and . . . [parts of Africa] are lost to the faith, those people who used to be Christian are now Mohammedan. If we had been truly Christian and let them overrun Europe perhaps . . . the conqueror could have been conquered, overcome by the sermon on the Mt.

DOROTHY'S VIEWS AND SOME THEOLOGIANS (Notes. August 21, 1960)

How hard it is to talk of these truths about Christ's teaching—peace and modern war, work, man and the state, etc. They [some theologians] do get angry as theologians. I too can see all sides—all problems involved. But Jesus' teaching is there. Even his apostles could not understand. We see through a glass darkly.

THE MYSTICAL BODY

What God has done for Christ He is going to do for us because we are in the Mystical Body.

THE SOURCE OF DOROTHY'S SOCIAL CONVICTIONS

The doctrine which is behind all our effort, the Mystical Body of Christ.

Part Three

THE SIXTIES

After her meeting with Peter Maurin in December 1933, Dorothy's work was set on the course it would take for the rest of her life—which would be for nearly a half century more. She was thirty-five years old then, a forceful, dominating personality with a touch of brass in it. Savoring her language sometimes were words like "hell" and "damn." A heavy smoker, she sometimes further assumed the pose of the hard-driving journalist by putting her feet up on the desk where the *Catholic Worker* was being laid out. If it was a pose, it was an attractive one, for young people came to the Catholic Worker house of hospitality on Mott Street to help with the work. Some were so caught by her radiant energy and vision that in one way or another their entire lives bore the mark of the special kind of dedication they got from her.

World War II intruded its harsh necessities into the exuberant idealism of Dorothy's youthful associates, who were then operating thirty or more houses of hospitality throughout the country. With the war, Peter's ideas—his agrarian program and his calls for a scriptural, personalist hospitality for the poor, which had seemed so appropriate in an era of depression—lost the vitality which the urgency of the depression had given them. Where Dorothy was concerned, the issue of the moment was to resist the war by preaching the gospel of peace.

Had there ever been a time before when a nation confronted war with such a total conviction of its moral rectitude as did the United States on the evening of December 7, 1941? Some of the bright young people of the Worker community made their "hard decision" (with some prompting from the draft boards) and went off to war. Some, however, convinced of the rightness of Dorothy's position, did not go, choosing, with its penalties, some form of alternative service. This division within the community was deep. The Catholic Worker movement began to crumble. Against the lofty passions that built up around a war almost universally regarded as utterly righteous, Dorothy's position was seen by many readers of the *Catholic Worker* as an irritating show of conspicuous iconoclasm, an embarrassment to the Church.

After the war the institutionalized form of Peter Maurin's and Dorothy's work took on a new vitality. In the altered perspective of things, caused by the use of the atomic bomb, to a lot of people peace did not seem to begin in the triumphal spirit of a conviction that the world had at last and forever been put aright, but seemed to stand, naked and bleeding, on the edge of a precipice at the foot of which lay the "lake of fire."

Religion appeared to move to the forefront of intellectual respectability and interest. It was said that a bomber pilot, or maybe several, had entered monasteries. At Mott Street, at least, one pre-war member of the community, Jack English, a bomber crewman, returned to his old work and then entered the Cistercian order. A vigorous life reappeared in the paper, the *Catholic Worker;* at the house of hospitality on Mott Street; and in the farms at Newburgh and on Staten Island.

Immediately after the war it seemed as if those who stood as the arbiters of popular culture tried consciously to return to the character of life just before the war's beginning, including that upsurge of sentimental romanticism that came with the first years of the war. The big bands were heard for a while and the world somehow lived without television. But the old mood was dead. Not only had the war reduced human life to an expendable commodity, to be disposed of with contempt; it also seemed to have dried up those sources which had brushed the decade of the thirties with lingering signs of romance. When ever again would a high school dance end with the playing of Ray Noble's "Goodnight Sweetheart?" And, increasingly, when those signs, as sometimes happened, reappeared, they, too, were treated with contempt. Some engine of ruthless change was at work at the heart of life, obliterating the past and, more and more, infusing into the air people breathed an insatiable craving for change, for a medium that would conduct to their senses the enlarging power of time's pulsebeat. The enrapturing sign of the moment was not a love lyric, done up in the caressing velvet of Frank Sinatra's warbling sighs, but the low-hung guitar, the message communicated in strident sound and sweat-producing contortions.

In 1960 Dorothy and her friends decided to sell the Peter Maurin farm on Staten Island and buy another with more land and further removed from the city. By 1963 all of this had been accomplished. The new place was an old resort center on the Hudson River, just out of Tivoli, New York. It was a beautiful site, high over the river, across from which the mountains, when evening came, would cast their long shadows over the water. There was a spacious lawn and several dozen acres of land for arbors, fruit, and vegetables. In front of the main reception center, built sometime in the twenties, was a second building, a majestic old mansion, gaunt and frazzled, but still able to evoke images of surreys beneath the portico and the spacious life of the Hudson River aristocrat.

The place, no doubt, touched squarely that large store of romantic fancy in Dorothy's nature. She was sixty-six years old at the time of the move to Tivoli, and perhaps she thought of the new acquisition as the idyllic location for her golden years, a place for conferences, retreats, and meetings—a place, even, of peace and order, conditions that previous farms never seemed to have attained.

Just as they had in the beginning, dedicated young people joined the community to help with "the work," as Dorothy would say; and the anticipated retreats, conferences, and meetings were held, and they did provide some of the high moments in the history of the Tivoli farm that Dorothy had hoped for.

But something dark and disturbing began to intrude into the community. By the sixties, a new generation, born in the shadow of the war and caught in the momentum of a change and flow that seemed headed for the stars, thought that by surrendering to that momentum the past could be left forever. The spirit of the new age had nothing to do with eternity; it was given over to time, for out there, somewhere, relieved of the weight of the past, was another paradise, the paradise of sense, and freedom was in the throwing off of all restraint to pursue this end.

No doubt, the failure of some vital part in the process of history had produced this new readiness to deny the past. Religion had failed —history had failed—so what blame was there in taking radical leave of what had been?

The emergence of the "cult of youth" after the war was a phenomenon similar to one that had occurred after World War I. Then, as after World War II, there was a denial of the past—a position that came out of a conviction, narcissistic in character, that the past had betrayed those about to face life. After World War II, however, this break was much greater than it had been after World War I. World War II more profoundly underwrote the response of "failure" where the past was concerned. But more than this, the war marked a time of dramatic acceleration in the process of change. It seemed no longer possible to maintain an organic unity between the past and the present. Futurism suddenly became the route of escape. The past was only a carcass, to be picked over largely for what mordant contributions it could make to the theme of failure.

No one understood better than Dorothy the cause for the "revolt" of the sixties, but as she saw it, the past could not be denied. It *had been—it was*. And what was occurring, borne on a wave of idealism, was not a "revolt" but an extension of the principle of self and sense beyond traditional restraints. There was still death on the battlefield, still extermination programs, and still a ravaging of nature. But more than these, the new hedonism brought death under a new guise: the maiming and death of tradition, which itself, in subtle and incomprehensible ways, held the potential for physical death.

Dorothy witnessed this development with foreboding. The past was of life; great creative work had been done in thought and art, a work that testified to truth and beauty and whose spirit had become a part of traditions that had imparted the "good" into the substance of life. The denial of the past could only be madness because its consequences were disastrous. A "climate" no longer existed that could lift the mind and spirit to beauty. It was a climate charged with sense. It had become the great perversion.

Though history had failed, it could not be dismissed. The roots of life were there to be nurtured rather than destroyed. The conduits of a learning and a tradition that gave meaning to life could not be severed. They were the sources of beauty, and to discard them for sense values alone as the end of life was to descend into hell.

At Tivoli, it seemed to Dorothy that never before had the problem of the lacerated and aberrational personality been so pervasive and threatening as it was at the farm. Where these people came from, and how they happened to end their wanderings there, was never clear. They created a community of their own and lived aside from what Dorothy would have had as a life of instruction, prayer, and worship. They demonstrated their separateness by abandoning all the traditional restraints which in past times had defined the canons of respectable morality. Many of them bore a disposition to regard Dorothy as a pious anachronism and they contributed to the practice, which began during these years, of murmuring against her. An atmosphere of confrontation, even hostility, on the part of some of the "guests" made a parody of community.

The war in Vietnam added its weight of grief to her life, made personal by the combat experience in it of her grandson, Eric Hennessy. And added to these things, it seemed to her that the spirit and the way to a re-creation of life and society that she had gotten from the retreats had been laid waste by the burgeoning new spirit which would have "all" in sense and power. The era for her was something of a dark night.

In some respects, however, the decade of the sixties was, from an outward view, the high point of her life. She was sought after for speaking engagements; she traveled widely; she was a persuasive voice in the peace movement; and she was the subject of admiring newspieces by journalists, who perhaps were taken by her supposed confrontational attitude toward church "authority."

Despite these surface signs of felicity, there were times when a deep sense of desolation burdened her.

YOUTH

PRAYING FOR YOUTH (Notes. February 3, 1972)

The subject of this statement is obviously the "guests" of the Tivoli farm.

I spend my days praying in the depths of my heart for our young people. Turning to reading (Pope John, Archbishop Bloom, Psalms, Imitation [of Christ]) . . . reaching out for help in all directions. "The sorrows of my heart are multiplied." I am afraid and my only courage is Christ.

There is an element of the demonic in the air we breathe these days. Letters come daily from parents who flee the cities with children . . . to escape, and evil is everywhere in the guise of sex and drugs, and words—"beautiful"— "love"—the "new family"—etc. Much lying and deceit, self-justification—an arrogant taking-over, a contempt for the old people, or tradition. They demand support, other people's work, to enable themselves to keep going. If refused, the ugly face of hate and violence is revealed, to subside into silent pride, arrogance, once more. "We know what we are doing. We are building a new order." What a parody of what we ourselves are trying to do. Self-discipline, self-denial, voluntary poverty, manual labor, washing the feet of others—they taunt us with all these things, blind to every need around them outside of their own circle, their own age group. They accuse us of every failure—to cope with drunkenness, insanity, and violence. "You have thrown out this one, that one. Where are the blacks, the Puerto Ricans? There is no democracy here." My heart aches for them, they are so profoundly unhappy. Their only sense of well-being comes from sex and drugs, seeking

to be "turned on," to get high, to reach the heights of
awareness, but steadily killing the possibility of real joy.

O God come to my assistance. Lord make haste to help
us. Lord, hear my prayer. Let my cry come to Thee. In
Thee have I hoped; let me never be confounded. All I have
on earth is Thee. What do I desire in heaven beside Thee?
And that "they" should have Thee, find Thee, love Thee
too, those you have given us, sent to us, our children. . . .
May they cry out for the living God. No one comes to the
Father but thru me." You have said this, Jesus. Draw them,
I beg you. I plead with you so that they will run to the odor
of your anointments, so that they will taste and see that the
Lord is sweet. Let them seek and find the way, the truth,
the light.

[Then Dorothy consoles herself with a quotation she ascribes to Pope
John.]

"Everything has its values, illnesses, crosses and tribula-
tions, provided they are borne in a spirit of faith in our
Blessed Jesus, who suffered for us and has promised us his
consolations and blessings."

YOUNG PEOPLE WHO LEAVE THE FAITH (Notes. September 26, 1966)

[Dorothy introduced this reflection with an approving
comment on] Pope John's great and trustful gesture, opening the windows. Catholics have been so complacently
apart, as a whole. No contact with the outer world. Gerry
Griffin [one of the young members of the Worker community just before World War II] used to say we at the CW
were protected and talked of getting out into the world,
meaning perhaps the world of earning one's living, too.
One is so well cared for and comforted in the Church, in
spite of all our criticisms. . . . [But] Peter Maurin's emphasis on the Common Good, with believers and unbeliev-

ers, Protestant, Jew . . . [had made their own group more
open than most that bore the name "Catholic."]

Tamar [Dorothy's daughter] was surprised to find how
good people are, how many serve regardless of religion, and
begins to see how mediocre, how bad Catholics are, how
sunk in complacency, when, having true faith and the sacraments, they should be so much better. "What good has it
done them?" etc. etc. So without having studied their own
religion . . . [many young Catholics] lost faith in it, compulsory Sunday Mass, compulsory Holy days, compulsory
fastings. They have never been taught the motive which
Father Roy so stressed, the supernatural motive which
makes each act in life full of meaning, nourishment,
growth. They have given grudging service, no joy in it, no
obedience since it was compelled, and they throw off their
chains, as they think, and, then, "all is permitted." Satisfied
flesh, in youth, satisfied conscience. Senses are stilled by
content for a time. The conscience is also stilled for a time.
So my conscience tells me I am all right, so regardless of
denying the sacrament [of matrimony] they continue to receive the Host, if the Mass pleases them, if they have "felt
it," "made contact with others." They have turned to others with human love, to their brothers, and this has become
a light which has blinded them, temporarily, one hopes. In
our group of young ones, they find love in each other, [or]
. . . in the poor—those of them who serve the [bread]line
for instance. But only those poor they *see* around them.
They give up confession but receive. They "feel" they are
right so they are right.

Meanwhile they despise the old, who have made such a
mess of the world, and with the old, the ancient, Church
itself.

DOROTHY, WEARY AND WORN (Notes. February 21, 1972)

[I am worn down] because I have been harried . . . all day yesterday by a consciousness that we were inundated by an ocean of unemployed and unemployable, black and white human beings, searching for food, warmth, comfort, and a momentary surcease from suffering. If you have ten volunteers working at the Catholic Worker, each one multiplies the load in the vain attempt to help, to satisfy one or another need. With the pressure of some of the most serious problems, I went to bed, aching in soul and body, sleepless for hours, keeping an involuntary vigil. I comfort myself by St. Angela of Foligno's statement that such sleeplessness, loss of appetite, and suffering . . . [is] not a willful asceticism that has little merit, but since it has no element of self-will and means only patience and endurance, it is more pleasing to God and more profitable for souls.

I see however that much confusion is the result of our willfulness, everyone seeking his own solutions, a refusal to exercise authority, a refusal to exercise obedience and humility. As it is, each brings more into the house, into the evening meal than we can feed or house. . . . Even when we cook for ten more than we expect, there is still not enough. The cold winter, the lateness of the month, the . . . group coming in (because they like our atmosphere) all make our evenings chaotic.

THE TRIAL OF BOBBY SEALE AND A REFLECTION ON THE USE OF FOUR-LETTER WORDS

Seale, a black, was tried for conspiracy for his role in the violent demonstrations attending the Democratic Convention in Chicago in 1968.

For how many days now, have we been waiting on the jury's verdict in the conspiracy case in Chicago, and how shocking a trial that has been. First the chaining and gagging of Bobby Seale to his chair in the courtroom and finally his sentence of six years for contempt of court. How terrible a situation we are all in with respect to the black. What a breakdown of all order and how helpless Judge Hoffman showed himself in the face of the violence and contempt of Bobby Seale. . . .

There was no possibility of introducing an atmosphere of "love of brothers," "love of enemy," into that courtroom. No good to remember "where there is no love, put love and you will find love." They were all on the rack, judge and defendants and witnesses and bystanders. . . . Could there ever have been a chance at mutual respect? It seems to me love and respect go together. . . . It seems to me that all who were listening in were taking sides, or in conflict themselves, trying to overcome their own wrath, and the whole procedure was tied up with the war in Vietnam —the horror of our being there and the helplessness of the young men in the face of the increased and ever increasing momentum of the State and the military. . . .

I have myself been at enough demonstrations, parades, marches of protest these past few years to know that in all of them were groups carrying inflammatory slogans on their signs, and pigs' heads and how there was always heard the shouting of four-letter words which by now have lost all their meaning. I myself cringe before such words because of the contempt and hatred they express and their involving the perversion of the act of creation. To use such a word is to drag the sacred and the beautiful into the mire. The love of God for man and man for God is portrayed in the Song of Songs. In the book of Hosea sex is compared to the love which involves . . . mind and soul and body and implies an act, a physical act which results in the miracle of creation. Looked at from a natural or supernatural aspect it is an astounding thing, and its sublimation has resulted in masterpieces of music, literature, and architecture. There are also the small tendernesses that are so much a part of love, of all loves—the tender love that makes endurable so much of suffering in this world.

It is hard to talk of these things. What I am trying to say is that the use of the word coarsely or humorously applied to the sexual act is calculated to enrage. There can even be said to be an element of the demonic in it.

PROBLEMS AT THE FARM (Notes. February 3, 1969)

I need to be comforted. We are the offscouring of all, as St. Paul said. To live in the midst of alcoholics, many of whom steal to satisfy their craving—and to have an alcoholic priest visiting us, and a drunken prostitute living with us, who has been in and out of mental institutions and jails—always released, over and over, always returning, plying her trade in our midst—only "she gives it away," as another prostitute said once—these things are so hard, so desperately hard to live with, especially for one "having authority," as the saying is.

But we are not to judge. We are to forgive 70 × 7. We have the parable of the prodigal son told to us by Jesus Himself. Of course he returned to his father because he was hungry and tired of his job of feeding swine. But who knows whether he did not get bored at home and get some more out of an indulgent father and wander off again.

Maybe that was why Jesus preached 70 × 7 and told us not to judge.

But when I think of this or that alcoholic priest, so fallen from so high estate, so filled with self-justification, so well dressed, well fed, driving the latest-model car, enjoying all the luxuries and comforts of a modern rectory in a wealthy suburb, I can only forgive him for his banal talk and most boring presence by suddenly seeing him as a victim soul. I'm sorry I have to use these old-fashioned expressions but I do not know how else to speak of it. He is suffering for the vast accumulation of self-indulgence and luxury of the priests and lay people who "can take it" and don't let it drag them down.

THE NEXT DAY: DOROTHY IS STILL DISTURBED (Notes. February 4, 1969)

I woke up at 7. Often I find that I have started praying before I am really awake, just as I fall asleep praying, Lord Jesus, have mercy on us sinners—over and over. Usually I am praying in a state of desperation—certainly not peacefully and confidently as I should. That is to say, during these particular days. So I come back to praying for myself. But it is the misery of waking to the thought of a drunken priest in our midst. Oh God have mercy on Father John. Pope John, pray for him. The priest's name is not John but there are so many Johns I'll call him that and be praying for all priests with their well-stocked bars. "Don't be Jansenistic, Dorothy." "Don't be prudish."

I'm despairing over drunken John and whorish Mary who said, "I may be depraved but he is worse." Tolstoi said to Gorki, "I have whored a great deal in my youth." As we all have.

I must read Osee or Hosea again. God's mercy and loving kindness, forgiving all, generous to all.

Sin is attractive in the young, and to the young. "The

call of the flesh is so strong then," an old priest said to me.
. . . Pope John XXIII pray for our priest here. St. An-
drew pray for him. Péguy [Charles, French poet] pray for
him.

WOE IN THE CITY

Dorothy, upset, writes an indignant letter. April 9, 1962. (Among
selected papers provided author by Dorothy Day, May 1975)

Bea was one of the crowd in . . . [one of our apartments]
renting for $21 a month. She was part of a group that
"reversed all standards," turning night into day, clinging
together, a dozen of them, to the extent that they all began
sharing apartments, girls and men. . . .

[When they were spoken to about this] there was indignant talk about our infringing upon their freedom. I in-
sisted that we no longer pay the rent of the apartments they
were using, nor eat with us, as certainly people do not
support the Catholic Worker to support a group of young
ones who live from hand to mouth. . . . There were as
many as a dozen sleeping in her little two-room place, and
then finally the landlord padlocked the place and they went
over to the West Side, I understand, which I take it means
some loft in the Village. . . .

"The corruption of the best is the worst," as these young
people come from good families, have good education, and
have been given every advantage. Sometimes I don't wonder the communists wipe out the so-called intellectuals and
Lenin had to write to Rosa Luxemburg of the bourgeois
morality of the young. This whole crowd goes to extremes
in sex and drugs and then flatter themselves they are at
least not perverts. . . . Also it is a complete rebellion
against authority, natural and supernatural, even against
the body and its needs, its natural functions of childbear-
ing. It can only be a hatred of sex that leads them to talk as

they do and be so explicit about the sex function and the sex organs as instruments of pleasure. . . .

This is not reverence for life, this certainly is not natural love for family, for husband and wife, for child. It is a great denial, and is more resembling Nihilism than the revolution which they think they are furthering.

THE SEX REVOLUTION

THE SUBJECT OF SEX (Note. N.d.)

After several million years or so of humankind's presumed ignorance of its existence, the generation of the sixties discovered sex. Dorothy reacts.

We look for happiness in sex, for pleasure, for ease, for fulfillment; and we lose it or spoil it in two ways: first by not accepting it all as from God, as a sample of God's love; as a foretaste of a new heaven and a new earth; by seeking such happiness as an end in itself. And second, by frittering away our taste for true happiness. If we eat always between meals, we have no taste for the banquet. If we listen all day to cheap claptrap on the radio we have no taste for the symphony. Our ears, our taste is dulled. And in these days when all the senses are indulged and catered to, there is a living on the surface, a surface excitement, a titillation, which never goes below to the great depths of passion. Even Catholics are affected by these attitudes toward sex. They indulge all the pleasures of the day. Music is savage, stirring the blood, movements of the dance are provocative, dress is immodest, pictures are suggestive.

When sex is so used it takes on the quality of the demonic, and to descend into the blackness is to have a foretaste of hell 'where no order is but everlasting horror dwelleth.' . . . Aldous Huxley in his *After Many a Summer*

Dies the Swan, showing the sexual instinct running riot like cancer cells through the body, degenerating into sadism and torture and unspeakable violence . . .

On the other hand, the act of sex in its right order in the love of life of the individual has been used in Old and New Testament as the symbol of the love between God and Man. Sexual love in its intensity makes all things new and one sees the other as God sees him. And this is not illusion. In those joyful days when one is purified by this single-heartedness, this purity of vision, one truly sees the essence of the other, and this mating of flesh and spirit, the whole man and the whole woman, is the only way we know what the term 'beatific vision' means. It is the foretaste we have of heaven and all other joys of the natural world are intensified by it, hearing, seeing, knowing.

SETTING PAUL GOODMAN [A CONTEMPORARY WRITER] STRAIGHT (Notes. January 18, 1967)

Paul Goodman said once, according to reports which came to me, that only [my] attitude toward sex was blasphemous —that he liked everything else about . . . [our work].

I believe as Jews and Christians [do] that God is a personal God, who created Heaven and Earth (the formless waste) and all they contain "in the beginning." All that He created was "good." It is a continuing process. "He sends forth wind and rain from their storehouses." He breathes life into the animal world. He is Creator. Man and woman are co-creators. In this lies their great dignity. Sex is in its pleasure, its joy, its "well-being"—the image thruout the Old Testament of the beatific vision. The nearest we come to God. Sex is a gigantic force in our lives and unless controlled becomes unbridled lust under which woman is victim and suffers most of all. When man takes to himself the right to use sex as pleasure alone, cutting it away from its creative aspect by artificial birth control, by perverse practices, he is denying "The Absolute Supremacy of the Creative Deity."

ADVICE TO A MARRIED COUPLE (Notes. N.d.)

The thought came to me this morning in trying to talk to you about your difficulties, sex between husband and wife is like food and drink for the satisfying of desires. It is for comfort and love as well as for bringing children into the world. When sex is only a receiving, a self-satisfaction, the penalty is repletion and satiety and a dulling of sex feeling between two people. When it is an expression of love—a serving of the other, a giving to the other, it keeps its sacramental quality. The sexual act, mutual, exclusive, intimate, is primarily an attempt to lose oneself, fuse oneself in the other. It is a constant renewal of the promise "They shall be one flesh." If there is not this sacramental quality—if there is just a selfish seeking of satisfaction, then the act is a sacrilege, a perversion.

If there is this sacramental quality, then sex itself, the contact of the flesh, should have a healing quality. There has been then a growth of understanding, tolerance, love and closeness. It is true that we cannot be happy unless we love, so it is worth making every effort to love. It is a question of deepest obligation for you since as a Catholic you have made this promise and you knew what you were doing.

THE MISCASTING OF SEXUAL LOVE (Notes. March 22, 1967)

Birth control, abortion, free love—all in the name of love. . . . The hunger for human love, how beautiful in marriage and in renunciation too. But it is always to be respected, even in all these free unions, even in all these sad searchings . . . [that are occurring here in our community].

BIRTH CONTROL

The following is a quotation from a paper, "The Ethics and Psychology of Neo-Malthusian Birth Control," read by Father Vincent McNabb in London in 1924. Dorothy does not identify the occasion of the reading, but she bracketed these passages with a red pencil and filed them, presumably for some future use.

> The Church has always had a most efficient method of birth control—by conjugal and virginal chastity. She has never urged what Neo-Malthusians say she has urged, "reckless propagation."
>
> To the present writer it has always seemed that some, if not many, of the leaders of the Neo-Malthusian birth control present the pathological features of erotic mania. The erotic mania tends to be a collective obsession. If there is such a psychological phenomenon as mob mania, it is time for us to ask if the present avalanche of sexual activities is not an example of this phenomenon. . . .
>
> It is only right to add that psychologically speaking, and insofar as economic or social states condition mental states, the spread of neo-malthusian birth control is mainly dependent on the present urban and industrial civilization. . . . We clergy . . . must do more than we are . . . doing to change this urban, industrialized civilization.

MARRIED LOVE

> If we crave human love, if women in their vanity can only love themselves if others love them, and suffer as they grow older in their desire for love; if it is love of which we dream

from our childhood on, it is most generally the love of men and women we are thinking of. It is the libido, the life force in us all.

When one loves he leaves father and mother and cleaves to his wife and they are one flesh. It is a love of union. I thought of this when my daughter who was young and shy turned so resolutely to the man she loved and was so ready to go to the ends of the earth, to leave me to whom she had been so close, only child that she was. I remember warning her one time as we walked down Mott Street and she was holding close to my arm, clinging to me as she so often did, that she must learn to be self-reliant, to depend on herself, to learn to stand alone. I probably hurt her by so saying. We are always hurting those we love. And at that, my advice was not particularly good. Man is not made to stand alone. That also is a Bible saying. It made me both happy and unhappy to see my only one go to another and cling to him and put him before all others, even if it meant never seeing me again. It did not mean that, of course. Fortunately, we have never needed to be separated very far or very long. But she was ready for that. Being ready is sometimes enough. God does not ask more of us.

A DREAM (Notes. May 30, 1957)

Last night I dreamed that one of the women from Koinonia [a Christian community farm near Americus, Georgia, founded in 1942 by Clarence Jordan, a Baptist minister] came and brought us an abundance of farm goods. There was a family of immigrants in the house, the man much younger than the woman. I knew he was not her husband and started talking to him, wanting to rebuke him in some way. He told me he was much older than he looked. . . . Then later in my dream I was on a train for Montreal and had misplaced my luggage and found myself going to make a speech in a soiled, unpressed dress and shabby stockings (wedding garment?).

MOTHERS AND BABIES

When a pregnant woman came to the community to have her baby, Dorothy's terms for accepting her were that she not place the baby for adoption after its birth but that the mother keep it.

> I am so glad to see the great happiness of the girls with their babies and they are to be congratulated for keeping them when priests, social workers, and all are opposed.

Dorothy once said that she was an adult before she was aware of the existence of homosexuality, a remark that was sometimes quoted to suggest that she was naïve where the subject of sex was concerned. Whatever her innocence of knowledge of homosexuality during the days of her youth, she got first-hand instruction from her prison experiences. The following comments are from notes made during her imprisonment following her failure to take cover during the air raid alarm of April 17, 1959.

PARTICULAR FRIENDSHIPS (Notes. April 24, 1959)

> How to write about this subject—shall we call it particular friendships? . . . St. Paul said, "Let these things be not so much as mentioned among you." But wars [and] slave labor camps . . . have led to a return of black paganism, a playing around—perhaps innocently at first, perhaps with a hunger for affection, for love—with dark forces. . . .
>
> We were put the last eight days of our sentence in a large dormitory, airy, tiled with old rose-waxed floor covering, with pink bedside tables, center tables, potted plants, showers (with curtains) toilets (with doors). . . . There were only twenty-two in the dorm ward which adjoined a dining

room where some graciousness was attempted by table-cloths, seldom used however.

Some girls missed the privacy of cells . . . for good reason—a desire for some hours of isolation and also for other evil reasons. [For example] on the detention floors there were two cells one could not pass without carefully averted head. At recreation on the roof where there were also game rooms for rainy days, and on the crowded elevators going to the clinic, roof, work assignment, . . . one could not help but see examples of utter depravity. There was one young very small . . . girl with short pinafore-effect dress, with a brown face and bright yellow bleached straight hair (a Lolita) and her companion who looked like a fourteen-year-old boy with a sparkling pink and white complexion, jet black hair waved in a ducktail hair-do. Of course she was over twenty-one or she would not be here.

There are three detention floors where there are many adolescents who are always supposed to be kept apart but who have many opportunities of coming in contact with the sentenced prisoners. The flagrant petting that went on in public between these two, the times I saw [them] wrapped in embraces, "he" with his face buried in the neck of the little bleached blonde, were innumerable and one would think would call for reprimand or the giving of "infractions" which the prisoners dread very much as they lengthen the days in jail. . . . Indeed many officers seem to find these actions amusing and laugh at them just as male-female impersonators used to be laughed at on Broadway.

These conditions are of course aggravated by overcrowding since practically all cells contain two which should certainly contain only one. The perverse cannot be isolated. . . .

There is also "friendship." One young girl who obviously had a schoolgirl crush on a sturdy young married woman who had two children, hung around her a great deal, begging for friendship [and] when the latter brushed her off too impatiently she complained mournfully—"I have nothing—they have taken everything from me—even a friend. One needs a friend."

I thought of a little pamphlet of St. Aelred on friendship, published by St. Anthony's Press, also of the friendship of David and Jonathan.

All love is a reflection of the love of God, just as all sin is perversion, a turning from God and a turning to creatures. All love must be respected. But evil is very close. The devil likes to simulate the good. He likes to offer what God truly offers.

LOVING HER COMPANIONS IN PRISON (More on prison life)

In trying to see Christ in our sisters, and loving them in their suffering, we are not oblivious to their faults—their sins. This should not be sentimentalism but true love because primarily we love them because Jesus loved them. He came to call sinners, to find the lost sheep. He even left the 99. He said to forgive 70 × 7. So we love them. We do not overlook the fact that they are, by nature, beautiful—brown-skinned, young, tall, of good carriage, strong, graceful. . . . I recognize the fact that "outside"—stupefied with drugs or ugly with drink, they would be hard to love. They showed us pictures of their children and their faces were alive with love and longing. Afterwards they lay sorrowful on their beds. But many times too they were triggered by some affront or injustice, screaming or flaring into temper or foul language, and their rage was such that others kept silent until their dark mutterings died down like the thunder of a summer storm.

On our detention floor there were 6 women waiting trial for homicide. They had stabbed or shot drunken husbands. One somber woman had hired another man to kill her husband for $100. There were those accused of forgery, kidnapping, shoplifting, assault, robbery . . . possession of drugs.

But there, mingling with them, all the day with gates open and corridor free, we were sisters. We saw in ourselves our own capacity for sin, violence, hatred. [As for myself, I] recalled occasions of temper, of throwing things that might well have led by "accident" to death. . . . And what dishonesty are we not capable of? All men are liars, the Bible says.

AND WHAT OF HER OWN PAST? (Notes. September 1946)

It took me a great many years not to wake in the morning and reach for human warmth near me.

When will I learn to love all men and women with the intense awareness of their beauty, their virtues (strengths) —to see them as Christ sees them.

Being "in love" is a sample of what love can mean in its discernment, in its "knowing" the other. A sample of the love of God. Intense, of body and soul, yet pure. "For Thee my soul thirsteth, for Thee my flesh longeth, O know exceedingly."

We are without sex, *all* of us, when we say, "Behold the handmaid of the Lord, be it done unto me according to Thy word."

OPENING THE CHURCH

On January 25, 1959, the peasant Angelo Roncalli, ninety days a pope as John XXIII, announced his plan to convoke the Church's Twenty-First Ecumenical Council. The first session of the Council opened on October 11, 1962, and in that and succeeding sessions the Church restated its mission in history in terms calculated to open itself to the critical scrutiny of all who were of good will. Dorothy, to whom the Pope was "our dear sweet Christ on earth," affirmed the purpose of the Council, but she was not in accord with all of the changes that came from it.

SOME REFLECTIONS ON THE CHURCH DURING THE COUNCIL (Ms. "Searching for Christ." N.d.)

It is hard to write these days because we are suffering from an embarrassment of riches in this time of the renewal of the Church in the modern world. New translations of Scripture abound. In reading over Paul's Epistle to the Galatians, which carries a subhead, "Faith and Freedom," in the New English Bible published by the Oxford and Cambridge Universities Presses, I saw again how applicable it was for our own day.

The turbulence in the Church today is a result of a new-found, newly realized emphasis on the liberty of Christ, and the realization too that we have scarcely begun to be Christian, to deserve the name Christian.

Everything said or written is challenged, new meanings and insights are sought and found in the counsels of poverty, chastity, and obedience; there is a new morality and a new theology. Old customs are being tossed aside as meaningless or offensive to others, in our deep desire for unity with our brothers of another faith, or of no faith at all.

A NEW ECCLESIOLOGY (Notes. July 8, 1967)

The new ecclesiology, of course, is not new—it is a rediscovery. The Church is an extension of the Incarnation, the continuation of Christology. The only Christ, the Mystical Christ, living on in the Christian in another mode.

This new self-understanding of the Church is simply beautiful. We should have had this a long time ago. . . .

We are the Church . . . the People of God, to use a Judaic
term. We should go back again and again in the study of
the Church. We will not stop at Augustine or the patristic
fathers but go to the Jewish fathers, the Church of the Old
Testament.

THE LITURGY (Notes. N.d.)

Just coming from church as I am, I am thinking of some of
my present criticisms about the new liturgy. Let me say at
once that to me the tremendous thing is the worship of
God in the vernacular, in the speech of the people. Even
the old Spanish priest is reading so distinctly that I can
hear the Epistle and Gospel each morning, though they
were the same old ones which recur year after year and
which most of us faithful churchgoers know by heart. We
have the privilege of listening to other chapters of scripture
which the priests may pick out but few of them seem to get
around to taking the time to find them. But these words of
scripture may be the same day after day but suddenly, just
as in the psalms which you may have been reading with
little attention, some words stand out, some fresh idea or
sense of the meaning pierces the heart with comfort. . . .

But let me get on with my gripes. . . . Now the altar
faces the people which means that you hear the words spoken in English . . . (but there is quibbling over the many
translations which have been offered). The priest faces us,
but in back of the altar there are three steps up and on this
dais the priest sits as on a throne, above the people, looking
down on them. It is the same in a number of other
churches I have visited in city and country. The saints to
whom the people address themselves in their loneliness and
sorrow have been moved to the back of the church when
they have not been moved down to the basement.

MORE "GRIPES." HEARING THE WORD (Ms. "Searching for Christ." N.d.)

The accent on hearing the word instead of reading it sometimes means that you neither hear nor read it because the celebrant has a cold in the head or the congregation coughs too much, or the celebrant races along at breakneck speed through the familiar words, and again they are lost to the congregation. I keep taking my missal along to Mass in case. Anyway, for me to take it in with the eyes as well as the ears makes a double impression on the mind.

And now even the prayer, the Hail Mary, has been left out of the listing of Catholic prayers from the new Dutch catechism, so we are told in our diocesan paper.

"MODERNIZING" SCRIPTURAL LANGUAGE (Notes. N.d.)

"Thou shalt" is an absolute expression. I cannot constantly be rewriting [words from the Scripture] in my mind, correcting myself. I still say these things over in my heart using the old King James or Douay-Rheims version of the Scripture.

The event of priests and nuns seeking release from their vows disturbed Dorothy. Her conviction was that once one had made a commitment to the good, a good that was not imperfect or wanting, one that could not be superseded by another that was higher or more exalted in its vision of human destiny, then a fidelity to that commitment was an exercise of the highest virtue.

PRIESTS IN SPORT SHIRTS (Note. January 10, 1967)

It gets so that when I see a priest without his collar staying
with us I wonder whether he is on his way out of the
Church. So much rebellion against the comforts of [recto-
ries and] convents. Going out into the world to see and
relieve poverty and returning to comfort. But the rigid discipline, voluntarily undertaken, enables them to do so
much work! In school and out, visiting hospitals and teaching children reading twice a week. How many ex-nuns are
doing as much? They are all afraid to bear the burden of
criticism which they will get, out or in. And they want the
appearance of poverty, not the secret practice of poverty,
mortifications.

LETTER TO A SISTER (June 9, 1970)

I am just answering a letter from a young priest, twenty-
nine years old, young enough, he says, to learn and grow,
asking for guidance and counsel who is in prison out in
California for protesting the war. He has been suspended
by his Bishop under Canon 2367, whatever that may be,
and he has given up institutional religion. So will write to
him and scold him.

And I do want to ask you to pray especially for two
priests . . . who both . . . are drinking priests and are in
a retreat house for priests a good part of the time. Every
now and then they are sent out to a parish and find themselves surrounded by priests who are able to take it, but the
example is bad and neither of them after some years seems
to be getting any better. At that, however, they are in a way
in a better state than a lot of priests who are so filled with
doubts and who are letting go of a great many of the most
beautiful teachings of the Church. These two are very good

. . . priests. It certainly is a mystery how the Lord leaves you in your weakness so often. I do feel that in a way they are victim souls who are bearing the humiliation and the suffering for a great many others who get away with it, if you know what I mean. I know that both suffer deeply, so I do beg you and all to pray for them.

A LETTER TO ANOTHER SISTER (June 9, 1970)

I can only greet your letter with the greatest sorrow. The older I get the more I feel that faithfulness, perseverance, are the greatest virtues—accepting the sense of failure we all must have in our work, in the work of others around us, since Christ was the world's greatest failure. . . . When you say you are going to join us, I can only say that within a very short time after you do that you will be most disillusioned with us (whether we deserve it or not is not the question) and [you will be] finding another apostolate. You will then wander from one to another—it is the usual pattern, and how little peace there is in this.

Part Four

OLD AGE
Letters to Friends

The society in which Dorothy's life moved during its last decade was of two parts. The first came from her work: the houses of hospitality, her writing, and her speaking. The other was the company of friends, people who in her latter years were not directly involved in her work yet who upheld her in ways that friends do—as confidants, companions, and sources of strength in times of trial. She had many friends because she was friendly and companionable. But Dorothy, on whom so many desperate and reduced people leaned, demanding not only food and shelter but attention and consolation, herself needed companionship and sustaining strength from others.

Among those who over the years she could account as friends were three who were especially close. They had known her from the time her vocational work began, and they knew her not only in her strength but in her weaknesses as well. They were friends because of what she gave them of her own self. They supported her with fare of both mind and spirit and even provided for her sometimes desperate need for respite from the cares and tensions of her vocational life. Within this circle was Dorothy's own family—her sister, Della, especially. Beyond this, there were three persons who supported her with a friendship that was based on a full knowing, one of the other, a friendship in which they gave and asked for nothing in return.

The first person was, of course, Sister Peter Claver—first, because she knew Dorothy first, and first perhaps because she brought Dorothy to the foundations of the spirituality on which the creative work of Dorothy's life was built.

The second was Nina Polcyn. Nina's contact with Dorothy began in 1934, when Nina, a journalism student at Marquette University, met Dorothy when the latter gave a talk in Chicago. Nina was immediately struck by what Dorothy was saying, and even more by the aura of conviction and purpose around her as she said it.

During the summer of 1935, when the house of hospitality was on Charles Street, Nina went to New York to help with "the work." The memorable event of that time for her occurred when some of the people of the house, Dorothy and Peter included, picketed the German ship, *Bremen*, to protest Nazi persecution of the Jews. The protest somehow developed into a street brawl, an affair which was climaxed by a vigorous intervention of the police. Nina, somewhat appalled, stood apart from the fray, Dorothy with her.

It was not the *Bremen* affair that sent Nina back to Milwaukee at the end of the summer. It was, no doubt, that she had appointments in Milwaukee, a mother and father who wanted her back home; but more than this, she could not dispel the feeling that the life of a house of hospitality was not her work.

As it turned out, Nina's work was the building of a successful Catholic bookstore in Chicago, Saint Benet's. From this position she was able to help Dorothy financially and this she did, almost without stint, over the entire span of Dorothy's life. Their friendship became very close, and what was the high point of this friendship—and surely of Dorothy's life in her latter years—was the trip to Poland and Russia that they made together in the summer of 1971.

The third friendship was in its character very similar to Dorothy's friendship with Nina. In the spring of 1936, young Leo Neudecker, a seminarian at the St. Paul Seminary, St. Paul, Minnesota, heard of Dorothy Day and, it appears, wrote to her to ask about her work. In any case, she wrote to him, asking if he might arrange a time for her to explain her work to the seminarians. As Father Neudecker wrote on July 1, 1983, "Dorothy was probably the first woman ever to give a talk in that Aula Maxima in St. Paul." While this event "did not exactly threaten any male traditions of the Church," it set some of the older priests to musing. The students, however, "all seemed to be greatly edified by Dorothy, and the whole thing did not hurt my image among my peers."

As a priest, Father Neudecker developed a strong social concern which took as its focus the conditions which attended and made wretched so many of the lives of people in Mexico and on the American border. It was his custom to take groups to Mexico and in the early fifties Dorothy was a part of one of his Mexican tours. Dorothy liked Father Neudecker for his uncomplicated priestly dedication, for his even temperament, his extravagant sense of humor, and certainly for his unquestioning and unconditional generosity to her work.

The selected letters which follow, from Dorothy to these three persons, are for the most part letters that she wrote during the last decade of her life. They show her increasingly succumbing to the physical disabilities that beset her and the struggle she made to overcome them. But throughout this frequently difficult time they show her faithful to the position, found in her two words "constancy" and "fidelity," that was the bedrock of her spirituality.

SISTER PETER CLAVER, NOVEMBER 4, 1970.

> Dearest Sister—I'll be 74, November 8. Do pray for me. God is good. Recent deaths (see paper) and sicknesses around here keep me home. But still I must go to the midwest [to speak] at St. Benet's [and in] Wis. . . . Father Hugo started it all, didn't he? But will get no credit.

Over most of her life, Dorothy seemed to be on the go, impelled in part by her love of travel—although, during the years of her vocational life, traveling and speaking were an integral part of the evangelization of Maurin's ideas. By the late sixties, however, travel had become increasingly burdensome because of failing health. She suffered from arthritis and an enlarged heart, the latter producing an increasing debilitation and symptoms which she called "flu." Yet in the summer of 1971 she, with Nina, made a trip to Russia which, from the standpoint of pleasure, was the capstone of all her traveling. The theme of the Russian trip is discussed in these two letters.

NINA POLCYN, n.d. [1964]

God willing, we will go to Moscow some day. Isn't that the cry of Chekov's *Three Sisters?* To go to Moscow!

But it will take me at 67 (in Nov.) 5 years to learn enough to read street signs.

Mike Gold says they treat arthritis down at the resorts for workers on the Black Sea. I'm afraid of planes, as you know, why can't you take a sabbatical and we go by boat to the Holy Land, visit Kibbutzim, The Little Sisters at Nazareth, and on to Odessa—then up the Volga to Moscow? Doesn't this sound entrancing? . . . I'll get an advance on my next book—borrow the rest.

TO NINA, MARCH 16, 1971

A travel grant from Corliss Lamont made the trip possible for Dorothy, but the problem of health momentarily intruded into the plans.

Here I am, laid up again—cold, flu, virus, pleurisy, leaky valve, breathlessness, pains in my right side (liver—lung?). It surely looks as tho all indications are I'm staying home —here at Tivoli, or rebuild it after my last year's travels. After all, born in 1897, I've seen a lot of the world and I'm not much longer in it. That is, unless I take pains to conserve my energy, sit in the sun, walk a little instead of being *propelled* everywhere. I would like to have ten more years to write, to live the life of a hermit, here in community. So, much as I love Russia, I'll use maps and guidebooks and literature to do my traveling, I'm afraid. . . .

I'm sorry to be a gloom. But I'm really ill. A "comeback" takes a long time. Much, much love.

FATHER NEUDECKER, JANUARY 1, 1967

In her letters to Father Neudecker, Dorothy's concerns were usually to thank him for his contributions to her work, but also occasionally to express an opinion on what she regarded as a misguided approach to the solution of poverty in Latin America.

I cannot tell you how happy it made me to hear that you were postponing your trip to Mexico until after Easter.

About ten of us have been down with flu, and it left me in a truly weakened condition. I could scarcely get my breath after walking half a block. I kept putting off writing you, thinking I would be better. . . .

I'm anxious to visit Guatemala and see the work you have started there. It makes me sick to see priests go all romantic over revolution. [One] . . . gives rousing talks in support of armed revolt . . . knowing nothing of genuine non-violence; wants to follow the tradition of priests leading armies in South America.

Every revolution has first led to another revolt down thru the centuries. People are losing sight of the primacy of the spiritual.

Excuse this blast.

Love and gratitude to you for all you are doing, so quietly—with so little fanfare.

FATHER NEUDECKER, FEBRUARY 3, 1969

Thank you, thank you! What loving kindness! Your gift came when the Christmas season was over and paying ¾ of our bills left us flat broke. At that we probably are not as much in debt as the rest of the world, the U.S. world, I mean.

I'm glad the trip is put off but I do look forward to a

future one, in the late Fall or whenever you say. I want to write about the 'little' unglamorous way of hard work, that the missionaries and local priests are putting in—the *non-violent* way, the slow martyrdoms and the need for U.S. parishes sponsoring mission parishes. But I don't know about Miguel Hidalgo. Was he one of the violent ones, leading a revolution which led only to more revolutions? I prefer the saints who are out of fashion now. So perhaps you won't want me along. . . . Love and gratitude.

FATHER NEUDECKER, MARCH 25, 1972

Father, a baker of fine bread, ground his own wheat.

Your flour arrived and it is delicious. We already are baking batches of bread with it and it is like no other flour we have had. . . . The only trouble is we eat too much of it! Would you mind telling me how much it cost to ship to us? I'll add to this letter what we have been paying for our flour—if I can get the figures from Beth who has charge of the farm.

What is all this talk about radioactivity in the milk and wheat of the middle west? My feeling is that we should be like the three children in the fiery furnace, singing canticles to the Lord. If we take up any deadly thing it shall not hurt us. . . .

I think it is noble of you to try to build this work up to help a school in Mexico. The worker is worthy of his hire, and the Church must be supported, but just the same, it is a warming thing to see a priest do such a work. You are a companion to St. Paul. God bless you and I beg you to pray for us all here, whom you have fed with fine wheat. Most gratefully in Christ.

FATHER NEUDECKER, MAY 1, 1972

Deo gratias and thank you too for your loving kindness. It is good to write you today—the anniversary of the *CW* which first came out on May Day, 1933—generations ago! I'll be 75 Nov. 8 this year.

Tonight we have a Mass here in the House in the dining-room after supper. All of the young people are neighbors, black, white and Puerto Rican. (A simple Mass, not one of these folk masses which I do not much care for.) I'm afraid I'm pretty much a traditionalist. We say the rosary (and compline) on the farm, and down here, Vespers. All the young here now get to daily communion at the 5.30 P.M. Mass, or the 8.15 A.M. . . .

Eileen Egan . . . is on our staff too and a brilliant writer. She has an analysis of Peter Maurin's thought as well as a story of Bangladesh. She has just returned from there. It was a joy for me to travel with her in India two years ago. No danger of the *CW* folding up when my "pass-over" comes, with people like her to keep it going. We've known each other since 1936. Much love and gratitude to you, dear father.

FATHER NEUDECKER, AUGUST 2, 1972

Eusebius fought the Arians [the Arians said that Christ was not co-equal with God—only an exalted human] and was exiled and was mistreated and went on [a] hunger strike in protest! Lots of Arians today. [. . .] says that he is so overwhelmed by Christ's humanity he cannot see or believe the divinity. Please pray for him. . . .

You were a dear to send me that present. I do have an account at the Red Hook bank up by the farm and suffer from guilt feelings. Some royalties go in that for my daugh-

ter who is poorer than any of us here. . . . But it is a close
family. . . .

Yes, I do thank you. I love St. Teresa's saying she was so
thankful a person she could be bought with a sardine. . . .

Hope you read the paper and all the better things our
fellow workers are doing. Don't get tired of our pacifism,
our seemingly futile work. I love to think of our pilgrimage
to Mexico. Love and gratitude.

FATHER NEUDECKER, NOVEMBER 15, 1972

Please forgive me. I've been ill for three months but recovering now at Tivoli where I'll stay hopefully for a year—
aside from little jaunts like to Nina Polcyn's wedding in
February. She is one of my oldest friends. And you are too.
So I'd love to get up to Minnesota to see Mary Humphries
and the women at Maryhouse in St. Paul, and you. But no
speaking anywhere this year. I've talked too much and too
long. Don't want to be a "garrulous old woman." Holy
silence. But you see [I am] garrulous even [in] this note to
say *thank you.* You are a darling, and I will do as you say,
draw on it for *myself* to visit grandchildren and
Tamar. . . .

DELLA SPIER, OCTOBER 15, 1972

Here I am, stuck in my room once more for a few days—
not answering the phone even. . . . But I am getting the
best of care. . . . Going down to the city for 4 days meant
coming back a nervous wreck—on the verge of tears all the
time, just from weakness. . . . Marge [Hughes] brings my
meals—I wonder at her strength and endurance. The work
would fold up (at least here) without her. But I'm sleeping
and reading, writing a few letters, and refusing to see peo-

ple. They come up anyway, and then I have to make an appearance just to stop rumors I'm on my last legs. Seventy-five seems a terrific age. . . .

Walter Kerell came up today . . . and brought me on loan [some] tapes—very beautiful: Bach, Handel, Vivaldi, etc. I'm looking forward to the Sat. opera.

I saw Mrs. Sheed while in town (she's 84) and she tells me *Persuasion* is Jane Austen's own love story. . . .

FATHER NEUDECKER, NOVEMBER 23, 1972

I've been laid up for the last two or is it three weeks with flu and feeling so lousy that every time I sit down to write letters, I get faint. That may be psychosomatic. . . .

Father [Marion] Casey was here (New Ulm) and advised me to accept your most generous invitation even though I did not feel up to it now. But of course it appeals to me mightily. Usually someone offering to pay my fare is what starts me out on a trip. And Eileen [Egan] is a marvelous traveling companion. But it is hard for her to get away too.

I am fascinated by all the approaches to work in Latin America. I'd love to be with you and learn about what you've been doing and what your friends have been doing.

We've gotten acquainted with a young Capuchin from Honduras who is working all alone in the mountains on just such self projects as yours.

What a contrast to . . . [those who want violence]. It breaks my heart to see this adolescent romantic infatuation with violence. I met an Irishman in the bus station in Montreal who was working in Brazil, on brief leave, who had the book about Camillo Torres in his pocket with my introduction—a very ineffectual one. He said that all the young priests are talking of Saint Che and Saint Camillo. I too admire them both but cannot help but mourn such wasted material and the terrible lack of the teaching of the Gospels in the seminaries.

Another thing. If I went so far, I'd like not to come back by plane but take a bus to California and visit [Cesar] Chavez who has visited us several times in New York. So if you'd take care of my fare there, and my subsistence in Mexico, I'd somehow get up to Calif. and back home. People would pay to get rid of me, send me on my way. In His love.

FATHER NEUDECKER, JANUARY 18, 1973

Your letter arrived this morning with its gift which was an overwhelming answer to prayer. . . . I'm at last recovering from the worst flu I ever had—began in August. . . .

Nina Polcyn, my old, dear friend is getting married Feb. 3 to a widower from Sauk City, Minn. I promised I'd go see her in late spring. There are lots of CW people around Minn. I'll borrow a car from someone and visit all over. Such plans. . . .

One of the things I'm writing about in my book "All Is Grace" is . . . all the wonderful priests I've known since my conversion in 1927. [And about] how I miss the old ways—Tenebrae, for instance, and Ember Days, and Benediction . . . and prayers at the foot of the altar and guardian angels and saints! When I'm driving around with Stanley [Vishnewski] on a shopping trip we sing the hymns to Our Lady in Latin so as not to forget them. They take so much breath that I wonder why my grandchildren have to go in for Zen breathing exercises. Oh dear. Please pray for them.

SISTER PETER CLAVER, DECEMBER 19, 1973

Had a wonderful 2 days with Fr. Hugo. He gave me good counsel. Feel happy and encouraged. . . . Fr. Hugo does

not like the new Masses on coffee tables and casualness—
etc. That's why he did not come to Merton House. But
these young sisters are lovely.

SISTER PETER CLAVER (N.d.)

I must say the new morality is depressing. How much sorrow is being laid up for these young ones. . . .

NINA, APRIL 3, 1975 ("At my sister's")

Here is some news. I got the Gandhi award, offered this
year by our old friend, Jerome Davis. It was bestowed at
the Unitarian Church on Park Avenue. Who was there?
Our old friend, our young guide [on the trip to Russia in
1971] who was so amusing. I gave a little speech of acceptance—about how dear Prof. Davis was, how valiant at his
age and how we had a wonderful time, young and old, and
what a good guide we had! And he was there and dropped
me a line, still guiding tours.

I am writing every day. My excuse for refusing speaking
engagements and so much travel. I really cannot get
around as I used to, tho I would love to. So writing must be
my chore. Much love to you always and to your dear ones
there. I hope your darling stepdaughter comes again.
Again, thank you!

Rejoice! Happy Easter time!

FATHER NEUDECKER, JULY 20, 1975

So strange—I had been thinking of you a great deal the
week before your most generous, even *overwhelming* letter
came (thank you, thank you!) because my dear friend Nina

Polcyn Moore had written from Sauk City begging me to come out and have a vacation there. Remembering all the friends we have in Minnesota, I specially remembered you. . . .

We still have the bishop's permission to have the Blessed Sacrament, thank God, and say Vespers and Compline each evening—8 of us. Our population is 70.

My spiritual reading now is Pope John's letters to his family, also his journals. He helps me a lot. . . . I would not be so tired if I did not try to see the many visitors who come. But I am doing no traveling or speaking for a while until the Lord pushes me to it. Do pray I get some strength back. . . .

DELLA (N.d. Ca. Spring 1975)

What a good custom little "bread and butter" notes are. . . . You are such a darling one—always taking care of others and making me feel so cared for. I always tell people how precious a sister is, I feel sorry . . . [for those who] don't have a sister.

There's a cold wind out today and the sun is shining and our house faces south so one can sit out, protected from the wind. I shall continue to follow the example set by Jane Austen's heroines and take my exercise *every day* with a cane. We may not have "shrubbery" as in *Pride and Prejudice,* or a horse as in *Mansfield Park,* but our legs are good enough for a saunter across the field with a cane.

I am reading *Barchester Towers.* You have a copy (by Trollope). He is first-rate. As good as Jane Austen, but a century later.

NINA, DECEMBER 8, 1975

An upsurge of strength has meant my accepting speaking engagements—the charismatics in Atlantic City (wonderful experience!)—a talk to the Eastern Bishops!!!—a visit to Alderson Federal Prison for Women in West Virginia with Sister Margaret Ellen Traxler and a group of Sisters and two women lawyers. Sister Traxler is head, I guess, of a coalition of Catholic, Protestant and Jewish women. I think they are trying to get me on their side (women priests et alia) but I'm just an old conservative. . . .

I saw my [granddaughter] Maggie and her "Oak." Mary, another granddaughter in Vt., has named hers *Forest*. Are they going to raise them Druids? Becky, the oldest, named her son Justin, thank God, one of the first Christians.

My main . . . [concern] is Helen Iswolsky's illness which is likely to be terminal. We are her family so I've been spending 2 days a week near her so I can visit 3 times a day briefly. . . . We are very close, so until she begins to mend, or until she dies, and is buried in the cemetery lot at Tivoli, I'll be staying close to her. She is my age, and I think closer to me than to anyone else. So I must stand by. . . .

It is raining and snowing out. Raw. Today is our anniversary. In 1932 I prayed at the Washington Shrine to the Blessed Mother to open up a way to work for the revolution! When I got back to New York Peter Maurin was waiting for me. I must telephone my sister-in-law, Tessa, to thank her for her Spanish hospitality. . . . God bless [brother] John and Tessa too. They made him [Peter] most welcome after I got back. . . .

Tonight we have Mass here at St. Joseph's house. Celebration.

NINA, DECEMBER 26, 1976

Your lovely letter and gift received. My memory fails—Did I thank you—for everything? "Our infirmities were multiplied—Afterward we made haste." (Psalms, somewhere.) I'm certainly not making haste with my bosom friends and well-wishers.

We have daily Mass here now—8–10 people. Maybe 2 go to parish church. Our dear and lonely priests!

NINA (N.d. Ca. January 1976)

I'm in the city this last month at least and so laid up with *weakness.* . . .

Cleaning my desk 2 letters from you a year old. Here another woman (she is just past college) and I are reading Chaim Potok's books. *The Chosen—The Promise* (I forget which comes first). He starts with 2 boys in Jewish households, school age, and such emphasis on the Torah, the Talmud, etc. Because of her interest this young woman volunteer in the house is studying Hebrew. (She is a good Catholic.) . . .

I had also read those mystery paperbacks about the Rabbi and from them learned more about modern middle-class Judaism. The Potok books are about the Hasidim, whom I had encountered thru Martin Buber's books.

Anyway I wondered if [my] having a half-Jewish niece or grandniece has stimulated your interest in Judaism. We really are closer, Jews and Catholics, than Catholics and Protestants, I think. . . .

Right now I'm in a feeble state. Too conscious of my 79 years! But Mother Jones, the great labor organizer, tramped the country from Colorado to West Virginia at a great age! . . .

Pray for us all, and for me that I get my strength back and can renew myself come spring in a little travel again.

SISTER PETER CLAVER, JULY 28, 1977

So good to hear from you and I do thank you for the *Ordo*. Remember how Jesus said "It is written, It is written, it is written" when he was tempted? I suddenly realized He read the Scriptures—O.T., and Psalms also. True God and True Man! Sorry to miss our retreats but I am "poorly" as the saying is. Travel and the excitement of retreats is too much. I am on the beach, very beautiful here.

NINA, AUGUST 12, 1977

In the "olden days" in Chicago, did you ever with other Chicago and Milwaukee CW's go to Msgr. Hellriegel in Missouri—outside of St. Louis, to visit? A great liturgist and a wonderful sung Mass by all the school children.

I'm on Staten Island, resting up and getting weary of it. Pouring rain today and doing my duty clearing up some mail.

NINA, OCTOBER 5, 1977

Your generous help went into the bank while I try to make up my mind what to do. I've been feeling so "under the weather," weak and depressed, lately that I hesitate to take any trips except to Tivoli where Deane bears up so valiantly in the face of her blindness. . . . I'm going there this weekend, I think. I am in the city now where we have such good help. . . .

NINA, DECEMBER 27, 1977

Did I send you a card already? . . .

Pray I get to be like "Mother Jones," I.W.W. fame, a wanderer in the 90s, so I can travel again.

Meanwhile reading is a joy. I am travelling with Charles de Foucauld in N. Africa now.

NINA, JANUARY 1, 1978

Woke this a.m. recalling our visit to Russia. What a treat that was. If I get my strength back, if—let's have a pilgrimage to London. Mary Durnin is living there for many years. Tamar and her youngest, Katy, are visiting for a week.

NINA, FEBRUARY 1, 1978

Tamar is spending some weeks with me and doing a lot of knitting for her *grand*children who are beauties. Her father, Forster, calls me almost every day and Stanley makes my illness an excuse to abandon the rural life for a time and be a gallant amongst all the young lady volunteers around here. . . . He and Tamar go for walks, exploring bookshops, and bring me back presents. This week it is a wonderful book on China. . . .

We have Mass twice weekly here at the house. The Little Brothers of Chas. de Foucauld are around the corner . . . and come and inspire us.

NINA, APRIL 4, 1978

You are a darling and I'm so glad you are going to Spain, Avila, especially. I'm still pretty weak, but go around the corner to Mass most of the week at 5.30 P.M. Sundays at 10 —a sung Mass by the Puerto Ricans in Spanish. We have the Blessed Sacrament at Maryhouse and have Mass here twice a week and I get to that. . . .

Pray for Tina at Avila. Or just keep her in your prayers. My brother John, born when I was 14 years old and still my dearest, brings his wife Tessa (Teresa) over on Sundays to see her sister [Tina] and drops by to see me too.

I'm still very weak but always have kept a diary, a brief one, you notice; lost them here and there, or goodly number got burnt up years ago when my bungalow on Staten Island burned. . . .

SISTER PETER CLAVER, APRIL 7, 1978

I've been ill—please pray for me—flu, exhaustion after a heart attack months ago—cannot seem to get my strength back. Can't make the retreat this year. . . . Also a feeling of jittery nerves! Shaking and trembling inside. Do pray for me that I do not become an old complainer!

NINA (October, n.d., 1978)

So happy we have a Polish pope—Wanted to call you at once to rejoice with you. Feeling lousy. Pray for me. I got depressed from seeing Elie Wiesel on television—Uplifted too! He is wonderful. Did you read *Night?* Love.

P.S. I'll never forget Warsaw!

NINA (N.d. Perhaps Christmas 1978)

A priest I met who worked on Fiji sent me these and I'm
using them now just because they are so beautiful. "The
world will be saved by beauty" is a quote from Dostoyevsky.

Stanley took these pictures—he's getting to be a wonderful photographer. I'm looking pretty pale, and I am, what
with that heart attack which left me weak for so long. . . .

We have a happy household here. . . .

About this card. There is a saying, "There is no time
with God." A priest told me when I asked about a suicide,
"All the prayers you will say *after* a death will have given
him the grace of turning to God." So we think of Christ's
birth and death and resurrection. Much, much love and
gratitude to you and yours.

NINA, DECEMBER 30, 1978

Do you remember Sr. Mary Eliz. Stanton, O.C.N.? She
stayed with us a while—those early days at Charles St.—a
time of Hitler! We hear from so many old friends these days
—holy days. . . . Early in the morning I sit in my window—freezing cold but wrapped in a blanket, sun coming
up, lighting a little this narrow street. A very beautiful
Xmas here.

NINA, MARCH 21, 1979

Here is our Polish pope [a picture], our dear sweet Christ
on earth, as St. Catherine of Siena called him.

Much love to you. Do write. I'm living a life of leisure,

plenty of volunteers, young men and women for both houses in the city and country. Sometimes I feel like a relic, treasured and pampered and spoiled "rotten" as my mother used to say. I wish you could see the luxury in which I live—large room and private bath. So much space it becomes a dumping ground. Where is my voluntary poverty? Two 5-shelf bookcases crammed with books, good and bad. Everyone is always giving me things of beauty. So I sometimes think that in addition to running a library, I am in a museum.

After my morning psalms and sticky oatmeal breakfast I am looking at an Australian illustrated calendar and remembering my trip to Australia years ago. Rome, England, Australia, Africa—surely I've seen the beauty of the world! God has been good to me! How wonderful it is to travel.

I have a shoe box full of picture postal cards, and Mary Durnin, formerly of Milwaukee, has become a world traveller—at least, England and Europe, and sends notes and cards regularly. . . . She sent me pictures of Rome and the new Pope—he is blessing the world. So good he got to Mexico, and blessed Castro as he flew over Cuba.

NINA, APRIL 17, 1979

Easter Greetings! We had wonderful Holy days around here, fastings, vigils, services packed in both houses, St. Joseph's on First St. and Maryhouse here on Third (all mail is at a local station, collected in the morning by Frank [Donovan] or "dear soul" Arthur J. Lacey whose vacation is always spent at a Trappist monastery). He prefers that at Conyers, Ga., where Jack English finished his days. We have always been so close to the Trappists, north, south, and midwest, and they were "activists" where we were concerned. They have kept us going with their prayers and as far as Gethsemane and . . . [illegible] N.Y. is concerned, with financial help. Also cheeses! Frank makes me a toasted cheese sandwich every day. I am pampered. "Joyous I lay waste the day!"

Did I tell you I hear from the Zarellas [Joseph and Alice, volunteers during the pre–World War II era] in Tell City, Ind.? And a fellow in . . . Montana sent a half dozen old pictures of when we were at Easton! And oh! how young and fair I was then! Vanity, vanity!

Give my love to Fr. Neudecker and send me a little card listing all the CW friends.

NINA, MAY 1, 1979

Remember Juliana of Norwich, "All will be well, all manner of things will be well" . . .

How many things to remember—Charles St., the Bremen and its swastika! And our wonderful trip to Russia. . . .

Time of change around here. We are selling Tivoli for a good price and buying a smaller farm at Warwich, N.Y., nearer to the city. . . .

I'll be praying for you and yours.

NINA, DECEMBER 18, 1979

Happy holy days! . . . Remember Jerome Davis, our guide in the Soviet Union? What a wonderful time we had. . . .

My good helpers, wonderful young volunteers just brought me breakfast. . . .

P.S. I was born in 1897. God has blessed me with a long life. Tamar's father telephones me every day. He is proud of his "progeny." Also Tom Sullivan calls, his voice as vigorous as ever. . . . Writing a book on Peter.

NINA, FEBRUARY 21, 1980

This was Dorothy's last letter to Nina.

Someone gave me these beautiful postals so I hope you don't mind my writing to you this way. . . . Got mail this morning from my sister in Vancouver who suffers so from arthritis that she has to dictate to her daughter. She has much pain. Thank God I am spared that. It's general weakness, loss of memory, too. . . .

We have Friday night meetings—a Dominican priest living with us. Mass 3 times a week in our auditorium where there are mattresses piled up in back, and often several old "shopping bag women" put [tie] on their purses, as it were, and sleep thru the Mass. . . .

I'll never forget our trip to Russia! And, of course, Poland. What good lives you and I have both had! Whenever I get mopey I remember that phrase, "Duty of delight." Much, much love.

Dorothy died on November 29, 1980, at Maryhouse, the house of hospitality for women on Third Street, a location that was within blocks of most of the significant occurrences of her life. She and her "darling Tamar," as she had referred to her daughter in one of her later letters to Nina Polcyn, were visiting when her overtired heart stopped. It was in the evening, just as the fading light was beginning to soften the harshness of the sights and sounds in the street below her window.

"In the evening we shall be judged on love," St. John of the Cross had said. These were the words which Father Hugo had emphasized during the retreats—words which for Dorothy had pierced whatever shadows seemed to lie over the course her life was taking. In her evening, one might believe that all which was of her mortality had been given to love.

Index